Poems of Hiromi Itō, Toshiko Hirata & Takako Arai

Poems of Hiromi Itō, Toshiko Hirata & Takako Arai
Asia Pacific Poetry Series 9

First published 2016 by Vagabond Press
PO Box 958 Newtown NSW 2042 Australia
www.vagabondpress.net

Hiromi Itō, Toshiko Hirata & Takako Arai © 2016
English translations, Jeffrey Angles © 2016.

Cover image © Miyako Ishiuchi (2016), *sa-bo-ten #18*.
Designed and typeset by Michael Brennan.

Except for on the cover of this book and the copyright information, where the names appear in the Western order with surname last for the sake of cataloging, all Japanese names in the interior of the book appear in the traditional Japanese order, with the surname before the given name.

All rights reserved. No part of this publication may be reproduced, stored in a retrieval system or transmitted in any form or by any means electronic, mechanical, photocopying or otherwise without the prior permission of the publisher. The information and views set out in this book are those of the author(s) and do not necessarily reflect the opinion of the publisher.

ISBN 978-1-922181-74-9

Poems of Hiromi Itō, Toshiko Hirata
& Takako Arai

Translated from Japanese by Jeffrey Angles

Vagabond Press | Asia Pacific Poetry Series

CONTENTS

INTRODUCTION 7

ITŌ Hiromi

FROM *ON TERRITORY 1* (1986)
Coyote 22
Vinegar, Oil 26

FROM *THE SHAMANESS AND HER INTERPRETER* (1991)
Father's Uterus, Or The Map 30
Marjoram, Dill, Rosemary 33

FROM *THE HEART SUTRA EXPLAINED* (2010)
The Heart Sutra 36

NEW AND UNCOLLECTED POEMS
Yakisoba 40
Eels and Catfish 42
Anpanman and Johnnies 48
Mother Dies 50
Cooking, Writing Poetry 54

HIRATA Toshiko

FROM *TERMINAL* (1997)
Greetings are Important 62
My Fun Family 63
Complaints from the Inhabitant 64
Weird 64
P-E-O-P-L-E 66
The Cat Stays Even After It's Gone, and I Cast
  My Suspicions on It 68
Can't Get Through 69

The Next Day 70
Lots of Visitors 71
The Vacant Seat 72
Upstanding Creatures 73
Making Up My Mind 75
Man Without Arms 78

FROM *TREASURES* (2007)
We Make It a Point to Wash Our Hands 80
Camera 82
Van Gogh's *Bedroom* as I See It 84
Lemons 86
Water 88
Treasure 90
Distant Sky 92
Morning Illusions 93

FROM *THE FREEDOM OF THE JOKE* (2015)
Beautiful Staples 95
At Some Point Things Get Rough 96
Do Not Tremble 97
Cold Spring 98

ARAI Takako

FROM *SOUL DANCE* (2007)
Give Us Morning 100
When the Moon Rises 103
Clusters of Falling Stars 105
Backyard 107
Colored Glass 110

FROM *BEDS AND LOOMS* (2013)
Beds and Looms 112
Galapagos 116
Half a Pair of Shoes 118

Lots and Lots 120
Specter! 125

UNCOLLECTED POEMS
Shadows 127

Translator's Notes 128
Acknowledgements 137

INTRODUCTION

This collection brings together three of the most startlingly original voices of contemporary Japanese poetry. All three are women who started their careers on the edges of the Japanese poetic world—a world that even now tends to prioritize male writers over female writers in the literary canon. Thanks to their bold experiments with style and subject matter, however, all three of the writers in this book have taken a place among the most creative and influential voices in the contemporary poetic world. Although Itō Hiromi, Hirata Toshiko, and Arai Takako take quite different approaches to their art, all are socially engaged writers who have used their poetry to explore the desires, expectations, limitations, and destinies of contemporary Japanese women within society, the family, and the workplace. This is not to say that they *only* write about the experiences of women—far from it. In recent years, Itō, for instance, has written extensively about the end-of-life experiences of various family members and about the experiences of the Japanese diaspora abroad. Hirata has written about a great deal about the functions (and *dis*functions) of modern families. One of the major themes of Arai's work has been the remembrance of people whose well-being has been sacrificed to the greater socioeconomic order.

Another commonality between these three poets is that they have frequently rejected the stayed, polished, and artsy language that dominates a good deal of poetic discourse. Instead, they have turned to the rhythms, patterns, and quirks of colloquial language to give their work a sense of immediacy and drama. All three have made use of various forms of non-standard, non-literary, colloquial Japanese as a source of inspiration.

A few examples might help illustrate. Since early in her career, Itō has drawn from the idiosyncratic linguistic patterns of people outside the literary world, and in recent years, the language of the Japanese diaspora has been a subject of ongoing fascination for her. The poem "Yakisoba" included in this anthology draws inspiration from the macaronic combination of Japanese and English—"Japanglish"—that she hears in the Japanese-American community of southern California where she lives. In her early work, Hirata often included bits of dialect from western Japan, the region in which she spent her early life. In recent years, however, she has moved away from dialect although she continues to pay close attention to the particularities of the ways that words sound, building entire poems out of sound-related similarities. Many of Arai's poems about the lives of women in the weaving factories of her home in Gunma Prefecture contain representations of the workers' dialect, thus giving direct expression to their woes and laments. For instance, the poem "Colored Glass" presents a modified version of a children's song, and "Beds and Looms" contains lines several passages rendered entirely in phonetic representations of the dialect of the town where Arai spent her childhood.

Considering that all three writers are so attuned to sound, it is perhaps no coincidence that all three are known for their dramatic and powerful readings. Itō's poetry, in particular, tends to gives a sense of coming from somewhere from deep within the natural rhythms of the body. When she reads in public, she punctuates her reading with bodily movements, fluctuations of the voice, and pauses that not only add drama, but also remind the listener that literature is as much about the sound of the voice as the printed word on the page. In her readings, Hirata emphasizes the sonic qualities of language, bringing alive the sound associations, alliteration, and use of homophones that give her work a visceral sense of direction and movement. Arai, who has written extensively about the theater director Kara Jurō (1970-), reads her own work with all the drama and presence of a professional actress, as if inviting the narrators of her poems to come inhabit her body while on stage.

Let me say a few words about each of the three poets individually.

Born in Tokyo in 1955, Itō Hiromi began to make headlines in the 1980s with a series of dramatic collections of poetry that described sexuality, pregnancy, and feminine erotic desire in powerful direct language. Her willingness to deal with touchy subjects such as post-partum depression, infanticide, and sexual desire shocked Japan—a nation that was until that time more comfortable with images of women as proud wives, mothers, and quiet care-givers than of deeply feeling subjects in their own right. Because Itō was so willing to write about these subjects, she quickly became one of the foremost voices of what came to be known as the "women's boom" of poetry in the 1980s. Although Itō frequently rebelled against the tendency of the male critical establishment to label her a "woman poet" instead of simply a "poet," she continued to focus a good deal of her attention on the kinds of experiences that, although common to many women, rarely became the stuff of poetry. A number of these early poems appear in *Killing Kanoko: Selected Poems of Hiromi Itō* (Action Books, 2009), translated by Jeffrey Angles. In fact, the title of the volume comes from one particularly infamous and frequently discussed poem in which Itō imagined killing her own daughter Kanoko in a fit of postpartum depression.

The poet Kido Shuri (1959-) describes Itō's position in contemporary Japanese letters writing, "The appearance of Itō Hiromi, a figure that one might best call a 'shamaness of poetry' *(shi no miko)*, was an enormous event in post-postwar poetry. Her physiological sensitivity and writing style, which cannot be captured within any existing framework, became the igniting force behind the subsequent flourishing of women's poetry, just as Hagiwara Sakutarō had revolutionized modern poetry with his morbid sensitivity and colloquial style."[1] The comparison between Itō and Hagiwara Sakutarō (1886-1942), a figure sometimes called the father of modern Japanese poetry, suggests the colossal importance of Itō's contribution to contemporary letters. In fact, many younger poets including Arai Takako (also included in this volume), Minashita Kiriu (available in another volume from Vagabond Press), and Ōsaki Sayaka (a recent winner of the Nakahara Chūya Prize for emerging poets), have all commented that even before they ever met her in person, Itō's poetry showed them new ways to write and helped to inspire them to write poetry themselves.

In the late 1980s, Itō's relationship with her husband Nishi Masahiko (1955-), a scholar of European and postcolonial literature, was failing, and she decided to go to America to start anew. One reason Itō chose America in particular was her growing passion for Native American poetry, which she had first encountered a few years earlier in Japanese translations by the scholar Kanaseki Hisao (1918-1996). The narrativity of these poems, along with their eagerness to use language in magical, even mystical ways, suggested to her a radically new approach, and in Native American writing, she found the tools she needed to rebel against the inward-looking, intensely personal writing of so many other Japanese poets. Her interest in Native poetry is evident in the frequently anthologized poem "Coyote," which begins this volume. In it, she describes the mystical connections across multiple generations of women in her family, and the ways that the transmission of language shaped their lives and sense of belonging in the world. As Itō mentions in this poem, her grandmother was a shamaness who communicated with spirits, and so perhaps it is no surprise that Itō came to believe in the mystical power of language. Itō's interest in Native poetry led her to the work of Jerome Rothenberg (1931-), the avant-garde poet who had published several key collections of Native poetry and helped make "ethnopoetics" a major force in contemporary American poetic circles. In 1990, Itō met Rothenberg when he visited Japan, and in 1991 she traveled with her two daughters to the University of California at San Diego where he was teaching.

Her stay in California was a turning point in her life. She settled into life in America, making friends and building a home, although her then rudimentary English meant that she maintained a strong sense of being a resident alien in a foreign environment. Since gaining permanent residency in 1997, Itō has divided her time in Encinitas, a quiet seaside city near San Diego, and Kumamoto, a city in the southern Japanese island of Kyūshū. Her already prodigious output of essays increased, and she began writing novellas. When asked about this shift, she typically mentioned it was because she was tired of the strictures of poetry and because she felt prose was better suited to exploring her new experiences as an immigrant. When she returned to writing poetry, the result was her masterpiece *Wild Grass on the Riverbank* (*Kawara arekusa*, 2005), which was translated into English by Jeffrey Angles in 2014. In this book-length and surreal narrative poem, she depicts the experiences of a young migrant who moves between two nations without ever feeling at home in either of them.

Several of the shorter poems translated for this collection build upon Itō's interest in the experience of Japanese expatriates and the destinies of their children. In addition to the poem "Yakisoba" mentioned above, this book includes "Anpanman and Johnnies," a poem about the students at a Japanese-language school in California; "Eels and Catfish," a poem in which Itō describes going on a search for the ancestral grave of Brandon Shimoda, a Japanese-American poet who came to visit her in Kumamoto; and "Mother Dies," a poem in which she talks about some of the hassles and identity crises that confronted her after the death of her mother in Japan.

A strong interest in Buddhism is another theme that runs through Itō's work. Since the 1990s, she has frequently drawn inspiration from *sekkyō-bushi*, a kind of half-poetry, half-prose moralistic storytelling form created by itinerant Buddhist performers. In 2010, Itō published a different kind of book, *The*

Heart Sutra Explained (Yomitoki han'nya shingyō), in which she provides essays, personal reflections, and modern contemporary poetic translations of well-known Buddhist texts. This book sold well, and she followed it up with a couple of other books pursuing similar themes. This renewed interested in Buddhism is one way in which Itō has been reflecting in recent years on the impermanency of life—a theme brought home by the death of her parents, her beloved dog, and the slowly failing health and death of her partner, the artist Harold Cohen (1928-2016). As a sample of this work, this collection includes a translation of Itō's own poetic rendition of *The Heart Sutra*, one of the most popular Buddhist texts in contemporary Japan.

At the time of the 2011 earthquake, tsunami, and nuclear meltdown, Itō was in California, far from the site of the quake, although she watched the news unfolding in her country with horror. Many poets, including her friend Hirata Toshiko, responded to the earthquake, expressing their thoughts for the nation through poetry, but Itō remained silent until 2012, when she wrote "Cooking, Writing Poetry" at the request of the *Asahi Shimbun*, one of Japan's largest daily newspapers. In this poem, she describes her own feelings of helplessness, not knowing how to respond, and instead, she expresses her admiration for her friend "Neko," the celebrity chef Edamoto Nahomi (1955-), who started bringing food to the earthquake victims in Tōhoku, then expanded her involvement by transporting food prepared in the disaster zone back to Tokyo, thus providing work to women in the evacuation shelters and fighting the fear that things from the region were contaminated with radiation. Because she was so compelled to help, "Neko" comes to represents an almost bodhisattva-like figure to Itō, who found herself not knowing how to respond. Itō uses this poem—an "anti-poem" in her own words—as a way to comment on the flood of poetic production in the wake of the disasters. After discussing some of the messages she sees in important Buddhist texts, Itō concludes that if language has a purpose in the face of disaster, it is to be a further the humanitarian mission of providing help and eliminating suffering in whatever small way might be possible.

Like Itō, Hirata Toshiko was also born in 1955, although she hailed from the island of Oki, located in the Sea of Japan off the coast of western Japan. She spent her youth in various sites in western Japan, including Shimane, Tottori, and Yamaguchi, and during university, she went to Ritsumeikan University in Kyoto. It was while she was in high school that she began to write poetry, earning the New Poet Award in 1983 from Shichōsha, one of Japan's most important poetry publishers. Her first collection *Shallots to Return a Favor* (*Rakkyō no ongaeshi*, 1984) was shortlisted for the H Poetry Award and the Hanatsubaki Award for Contemporary Poetry. Her second collection *Watery Atlantis Is So Reserved* (*Atoranteisu wa mizukusai*, 1987) was shortlisted for the Takami Jun Award, an annual award given to a work of important and innovative literature. Along with Itō, she became known as one of the foremost voices of the "women's boom" of poetry, earning a reputation for her ability to turn her own life, thoughts, and day-to-day feelings into poems that are both poignant and sometimes quite light-hearted.

In the year 1990, she settled in Tokyo, where she continued to publish poetry at a rate of one collection every two or three years. Her collection *The Fragile Odd Couple* (*[O]moroi fūfu*, 1993) turns the experiences of a troubled, married couple into poetry—poetry so direct and colloquial that one might even call it a collection of "anti-poems" for its willingness to break free of the kinds of reserved, understated language so common in the postwar Japan. In particular, it turns ordinary household conversations and conversations into poems, which allow one to catch glimpses of both the sensuality and the acrimony of the husband and wife. The unusual prosaic style of these poems, the quirky mode of presentation, and the glimpses of humor embedded throughout quickly captured the attention of a wider public. Perhaps it is not much of a surprise then that in subsequent years, Hirata tried her hand at writing prose, penning several short-story collections and novels, including *Piano Sandwich* (*Piano Sando*, 2003), *Two on Board* (*Futari nori*, 2005), *Getting Slugged* (*Nagurareta hanashi*, 2008), *My Soft Red Part* (*Watashi no akakute yawaranaka na bubun*, 2009), and *Slope* (*Surōpu*, 2010).

In 1997, a few years after her separation with the partner who inspired *The Fragile Odd Couple*, Hirata published *Terminal*, which won the Doi Bansui Prize for poetry and was nominated for the Takami Jun Award. This collection is not strictly autobiographical; however, the depictions of quirky, dysfunctional families reflect one of Hirata's recurring themes—the sense of unease that many people feel within the structures of their own families. In the place of her earlier, more colloquial style, this collection vacillates between straightforward language and formality, describing strange, threatening scenes reminiscent of Edward Gorey. In many of the poems from *Terminal*, including the poems "My Fun Family," "Weird," and "Complaints from the Inhabitant," all of which appear in translation in this collection, describe people in domestic situations that are far from idyllic. If anything, a sense of dread lurks in these poems, as if dangerous forces are working to threaten or even dismantle the household.

Many of Hirata's poems reflect the poet's strong sense of unease with the attention of others. As she has written in her essays, she is highly conscious of the ways that other people look at and think about her. During her youth, a burn left her with large scars on her back and on her arms, and as a result, schoolgirls bullied her and left her feeling self-conscious about her appearance. (It was only as an adult when the world-renowned feminist photographer Ishiuchi Miyako took photographs of her scars that Hirata was able to overcome these childhood traumas. Ishiuchi, incidentally, is the same photographer who took the photograph of the cactus on the cover of this book.) Later in life, as she describes in the poem "Lots of Visitors," her separation from her partner led to all sorts of attention that was not necessarily welcome. Rather than allowing her discomfort with the viewing, critical gaze to fester, however, Hirata has taken this discomfort and turned it into poems rich with black humor. Her light, humorous touch allows her poems to transcend simple self-pity, and it ensures that they succeed as small works of art.

In 2004, she won the Hagiwara Sakutarō Prize for poetry for her 2004 collection *Shi nanoka*, in which she turns a description of what happens to her on the seventh day of each month into a poem. Once again, her willingness to treat seemingly day-to-day thoughts, random associations, and small happenings mean that she ends up writing about subjects that are rarely the stuff of poetry. In fact, the title of this collection is written with characters that mean "Poetry on the Seventh Day," but the title is a homonyms that could also mean "Is This Poetry?" Quite literally, Hirata is challenging us as her readers to reconsider our expectations about poetry and what kinds of work it should do. (Hirata also chose the phrase for a title because it sounds like the evocative phrase *shonanoka*, meaning the "seventh day after a death.")

Many of the poems in *The Freedom of the Joke* (*Zaregoto no jiyū*, 2015), also treat small and intimate subjects, including the poem "Beautiful Staples" translated in this book; however, *The Freedom of the Joke* also contains a number of poems written in response to the March 11, 2011 disasters. Among them are "Do Not Tremble," first published in the large daily newspaper *Yomiuri Shimbun* on March 28, a little more than two weeks after the worst of the disasters, although aftershocks were still shaking eastern and central Japan several times per day. This poem represents Hirata's straightforward, heartfelt prayer that the earth would stop shaking and allow people's lives to return to normal. Since this poem was one of the first poems written in response to the crisis and because it reflected the thoughts of so many citizens through the country, it has been recited frequently and often appears in discussions of disaster-related poetry. "Cold Spring" was first published in 2015, the year that marked the seventieth anniversary of the end of World War II and the fourth anniversary of the disasters. In the poem, she remembers the losses in her own life and reflects on how she keeps those people alive in her own heart.

Arai Takako was born in 1966 in Kiryū, a city in central Japan known for textile production. Arai's father is the manager of a small, cottage-style weaving factory located on the family property. At its height, the factory employed a few dozen people and produced some of the high quality, finely woven silks that earned an international reputation for the region. Many of Arai's poems, including many poems in her second and third books in particular, focus on the lives of the women workers she saw while growing up. As Arai is quick to point out in her talks and essays, although women have been traditionally associated with weaving for centuries, women supplied the main source of labor in the textile industry since Japan started its rapid modernization in the mid-nineteenth century. It was also women who were most immediately affected by the collapse of the textile industry in the late twentieth and early twenty-first centuries as production was outsourced to developing nations.

Arai came to Tokyo for secondary education and graduated from Keiō University. She has published three books of poems to date: *The Emperor's Unfortunate Lover* (*Haō Bekki*, 1997), *Soul Dance* (*Tamashii dansu*, 2007), and *Beds and Looms* (*Betto to shokki*, 2013). Some of the poems in her second collection, which won the Oguma Hideo Prize, appear in English translation in *Four from Japan: Contemporary Poetry and Essays by Women* (Litmus/Belladonna, 2006) and *Soul Dance: Poems of Takako Arai* (Mi'Te Press, 2008). Arai was one of the founders of the journal *Shimensoka* (1992-1995), and later of *Mi'Te*, a journal that she continues to edit even now and that has stretched to well over one hundred issues. She has served on the organizational board of the Tokyo International Poetry Festival, and she has a growing international reputation as one of the most exciting of Japan's young generation of poets. Arai currently lives in Yokohama and teaches Japanese to international students at Saitama University.

Much of Arai's work is avant-garde, incorporating experimental stylistic features such as the incorporation of dialect, radical juxtaposition of images, and the frequent use of sentence fragments. At the same time, however, her poems are often far more socially engaged than the work of many other contemporary Japanese poets. She uses her poetry to keep the memory of the women workers she saw during her youth alive, even as the factories where they once worked are turning into vacant lots. For instance, in the poem "When the Moon Rises," she describes the ways that gestures learned while working in textile factories remain part of women's lives, even long after the factories themselves have been closed down. Similarly in "Colored Glass," she imagines the ways that the factory gets into the soul of an individual in even more literal terms—the poem describes a girl swallowing a silkworm so that her body literally becomes the factory where the silk is produced. In "Beds and Looms," the title poem from her third anthology, Arai describes the ways that the sexual lives of the women workers infiltrated life in the factory more generally.

Other poems have explored the ways that women's lives have been shaped by contemporary trends, including the push toward globalization and the economic downturn in the first decade of the twenty-first century. For instance, the poem "Clusters of Falling Stars," is a poem of protest inspired by Horie Takafumi (1972-), the CEO of an IT company who engaged in securities fraud and was put in jail for twenty-one months. In her poem, Arai focuses on the ways Horie's malfeasance affected the lives of ordinary people, even those who had little direct connection to him.

Like many poets, Arai felt the call to respond through poetry to the 2011 earthquake, tsunami, and nuclear meltdown in northeastern Japan. Her poem "Galapagos," written soon after the disasters, is one of the rare poems that uses an element of humor to respond to the problems. In this poem, Arai takes many of the issues in the Japanese press in the year after the 2011 disasters and synthesized them into an organic whole—the ongoing anxiety about the Japanese economy during the ongoing nuclear crisis at Fukushima, concern about the extremely low national birthrate, and even the lack of individuality of Japanese youth as manifested in the almost universal tendency to wear clothes from Uniqlo. In fact, in the wake of so much bad news in 2011, Uniqlo's entry into several new, major global markets in 2012 proved to be a ray of hope to the media, which seized upon it as a step forward for Japanese business and the economy. Given this publicity, it is perhaps no surprise that Arai singles out Uniqlo for particular attention. The poem "Half a Pair of Shoes," was inspired by a trip she made in the immediate aftermath of the 2011 disasters to Kesennuma, one of the coastal cities almost completely washed away by the tsunami. At the time of her visit, the shoes and clothing of the victims and other coastal inhabitants were still washing onto the shore. The sight of a single shoe lying on the shore becomes the starting point for this poem exploring what it means to be a poet attempting to reconstruct the stories of victims based on physical evidence alone.

Finally, the poem "Lots and Lots" was inspired by the commentary of several authors writing post-Fukushima about the ways that the Japanese population had become desensitized to atomic power, even though their experiences with atomic energy in Hiroshima and Nagasaki had been nothing short of nightmarish. She singles out the work of the manga artist Tezuka Osamu (1928-1989), whose wildly popular comic character "Iron-Armed Atom" (Tetsuwan Atomu) suggested to the Japanese population that nuclear power could be used for good. As Arai points out in the first stanza, the character's name was changed to "Astro Boy" when the animated feature based on this comic was first exported to the United States. Throughout this poem, Arai uses Tezuka's character "Atom" as a stand-in for the fifty-four nuclear stations located throughout Japan. The final stanzas riff on three classic modern Japanese poems: Yoshioka Minoru's "Monks" (Sōryo), Anzai Fuyue's "Spring" (Haru), and Hagiwara Sakutarō's "Bamboo and its Grief" (Take to sono aishō). By ironically and humorous rewriting these famous poems in ways that are relevant to the Fukushima meltdown, Arai shows the ways that the power of poetry—even poems already in existence—can be harnessed and rewritten to produce commentary in a time of crisis.

---

1. Nomura Kiwao and Kido Shuri, *Sengo meishi sen II* (Selection of famous postwar poetry II), Gendai shi bunko tokushū han 2 (Tokyo: Shichōsha, 2001), 230.

ITŌ HIROMI

FROM *ON TERRITORY 1* (1986)

COYOTE

My grandmother was a medium
My mother was a magician
My mother's older sister was a geisha
My mother's younger sister had tuberculosis
My mother's other younger sister was barren
All were wonderfully beautiful
The spells mother taught me
All required saké, rice, and salt
We were afraid of snakes, water, and the east

My daughter began speaking baby talk at two months
When the coyote speaks to her
She smiles and always responds
The coyote: *A dry plain, plain, plain*
My daughter: *Plain, plain, plain*
The coyote: *No lying*
My daughter: *No lying, no lying, no lying*
The coyote: *Hungry, hungry*
My daughter: *Hungry too*
Coyote: *Hah, hah, hah*
My daughter: *Haaaaaaa-ohh*
My daughter's father, my father: *I wanted to concentrate just on the coyote*
I wanted to isolate myself, insulate myself, see nothing other than the coyote
And I wanted to trade places with him

The milk flows from my breast bountifully
To fatten my daughter it flows in overabundance, much too much
My grandmother's milk also flowed bountifully
With it she fattened her four girls and two boys
My mother's older sister's milk also flowed bountifully

With it she fattened her three boys
My mother's milk also flowed bountifully
With it she fattened just me, and the leftover milk flowed out
My mother's younger sister's milk also flowed bountifully
With it she fattened her two boys
My mother's other younger sister nursed and nursed her adopted child
With her milkless breasts until eventually
The milk began to flow from her body
There is so much rain
Everything and anything gets soaked
Inside a damp frame, grandmother's beautiful smiling face with no eyebrows or teeth
My mother's older sister's beautiful face with no chin, teeth, or hair but with large lips
My mother's younger sister's beautiful face with fleshy, hairless lashes and no teeth
My mother's younger sister's beautiful face with spots and no teeth
My mother's beautiful face with sagging cheeks, crow's feet, and no armpit hair nor teeth
But all of them have breasts that sag

The women all enjoy fondling the babies in the family
My daughter
Is the only female grandchild
Is the only female niece

The words of the women who fondle the babies in the family
Slowly turn to baby talk before our eyes
The women from age ninety to fifty gather
(The ninety year-old has been dead for a decade)
The women sit together and
Begin to speak in baby talk
Gyaaatei

Gyaaatei
Haaraagyaatei
Harasoogyaatei

My grandmother was a medium
My mother was a magician
My mother's older sister was a geisha
My mother's younger sister had tuberculosis
My mother's other younger sister was barren
My grandfather was a paralytic
My mother's older brother died young
My mother's younger brother did not speak at all
My father was related to none of them
My mother's husband and my husband
Vanished right before
I gave birth to my daughter

Coyote: *Gyaatei*
My daughter: *Gyaatei*
Coyote: *Haaraagyaatei*
My daughter: *Haraharagyaatei*
Coyote: *Gyaagyaagyaatei*
My daughter: *Haragyaatei*

The precipitation and humidity this time of year
My mother chants her magical spells
Cursing the humidity
Saké and rain
Rice and rain
Salt and rain
Ordering the water
To flow to the east
Forgive us, oh honorable snake

Saké and rain
Rice and rain
Salt and rain

VINEGAR, OIL

Onions, eggplants, pork
Stir-fried onions, deep-fried eggplants, stir-fried pork
Round slices of stir-fried onion, purple backs of deep-fried
    eggplants, white bellies of deep-fried eggplants
Tiny dried sardines, grated daikon
Young dried sardines, vinegar, grated daikon
Tomatoes, radish sprouts, lettuce
Remaining tomatoes, remaining sprouts, remaining lettuce,
    vinegar, oil
Fatty pork, blackened konnyaku, daikon
Lotus roots, pork, oil
Fatty pork, deep-fried eggplant, liver
The glaze of the Shino dishes
Shiny black rods of something (can't tell what)
Soy sauce, whitefish, lettuce
Rice with hashed meat
Gooey onions, gooey beef, gooey rice grains
A mix of kidney beans, chicken, onions
Grease from the pork
Squid, mushrooms
White squid, shiny mushrooms
Shiny white squid, shiny mushrooms stuck together
Shiny white squid stuck together, shiny mushrooms stuck
    together and falling apart
Fatty pork, scallops
Butter, ketchup, ketchup
Patterns that come to the surface of the fried eggs
Pickled plums, perilla
Salt
(*Long life, love, fire prevention, safe childbirth, moles, removing thorns,
    deformities, childcare*)
(*Tofu, belt-removal, malt candy, falling off horses*)

I want to do these,
Show me,
I want to lick,
Tomorrow,
Better yet, today,
I want to breed,
I want to,
I want to eat,
I want to eat,
I want to eat,
I want to eat,
I don't care whom,
This is what I'm trying to say
The man I loved like mad likes sushi
So we went to sushi shops all the time
The man I loved almost to the point of madness got the same thing each time
The regular platter for two
Man and woman, mad with love
We sat across from each other in a corner of the sushi shop
And ate our regular plate of sushi
River herring, tuna, squid, eggs
I thought about trying to sit at the counter
Choosing the sushi up there and eating it with him
But another, plain-looking man appeared before me
We talked about sushi shops
Conger eel
Fatty tuna
Yellow clams, scallops, cockles, abalone
I thought if I were with him I could eat any kind of sushi I wanted
In other words, I switched men
We went out to eat sushi every once in a while
But I always ended up treating
If that was how it was going to be

It was about the same as going out for sushi all alone
So I made sure not to expect sushi from the next man to come along
I want us to love one another
Be in love
Really in love
Loving
Licking
Sucking
I want us to love one another
Be in love
Really in love
Loving
I want us to love one another
Be in love
(*Long life, love, fire prevention, safe childbirth, moles, removing thorns, deformities, childcare*)
(*Tofu, belt-removal, malt candy, falling off horses*)
Menstrual blood from my mother's older sister
Menstrual blood from my mother's younger sister
Menstrual blood from my grandmother
Menstrual blood from my mother
Soaked into cotton and rags
I understand they would stitch them by themselves
And when they got dirty, they washed them and used them over
And on top, they wore black underpants they also sewed
So they wouldn't be ashamed if the stain came through
Grandmother gave birth to my mother when she was forty
Mother gave birth to me when she was thirty
When I was born, my seventy year-old grandmother had not menstruated for years
I gave birth to my daughter when I was twenty-eight
When she was born, my fifty-eight year-old mother had not menstruated for years
When my water broke, dabs of blood came out too

Almost like I was menstruating
I realized that if I conceived before my next period
I'd create a child born the same year almost like a twin
But I did not conceive
Once again
I realized that if I conceived before my next period
I'd create a child born the next year who people might mistake for a twin
But I did not conceive
And my periods kept coming
(*Long life, love, fire prevention, safe childbirth, moles, removing thorns, deformities, childcare*)
(*Tofu, belt-removal, malt candy, falling off horses*)

FROM *THE SHAMANESS AND HER INTERPRETER* (1991)

FATHER'S UTERUS, OR THE MAP

In that room various body parts
Are stuffed into various bottles
We saw various deformities, various strange diseases
We could have seen various dead bodies but
The men didn't want to go there
That's why all I saw were parts of bodies
Body parts that had changed color in the liquid
No chance
Of them coming back to life

Look, that's my father's arm
The men said pointing to an arm all dried up
That's my father's skin
The men pointed to a patch of skin ridden with disease
That's my father's stomach
The men pointed to a stomach with ulcers
Those are my father's testicles
The men pointed to testicles with elephantiasis
Those are my father's bones and spinal column
Those are my father's joints
Those are us, the children our father gave birth to
The men pointed to fetuses with hydrocephalus
And that is you
The men pointed to a breast with cancer
And that is my father's uterus
The men pointed to a uterus that had grown teeth
There were a row of teeth pushing the flesh aside
I wanted to say
This is a disease, a deformity

But I did not
That is my father's uterus
When we were boys, our father often thrashed us
Those are the cruel uterine teeth that punished us
One began to sob
Another began to dance
Meanwhile the men suddenly broke the bottle
With the uterus with the teeth
Regardless of whether it was their father's or anyone else's
Regardless of whether it was the result of disease or deformity
The bottle broke
Tears and medicinal fluid
Teeth and glass shards
I thought
These actions are merely maudlin
But I did not say anything
"When I open the map and think about where I want to go
There is my father, standing everywhere on the map
I become desperate to find someplace he's not
My father stands everywhere
My father stands everywhere on the map, I point and he's there"
I am telling this story I heard somewhere of father and daughter
When one of the men gives me a map
A map marked in a foreign tongue
I know the contours of the land
I know the names of places too but
I can't read the language
The men can read it however
So whenever I look at the map
That language
The men who read that language
Watch me with tactful eyes

Of course the man who gave me the map

And immediately started to stand watch
Regretted his actions
He writhed with regret
Be quiet (I wished)
Drop dead (I wished)
He should die the dullest death imaginable
Dashing chewed gum to the floor or
Disappearing suddenly in a burst of wind or
Starving to death or something
Still the man gives me a map in order to keep watch
No matter when, no matter where, he is standing there in the map
He appears even inside the bottles, come back to life
But the man regrets
He writhes with regret
No choice but to leave him be
Call out and
Immediately he is standing there
He is going to thrash me
The man's blood vessels brim to overflowing
The same way they have dozens, hundreds of times
Father, older brother
Husband, lover, teacher, whatever I call him

MARJORAM, DILL, ROSEMARY

The pleasure of another's embrace is so strong
I want nothing more
Even though situations change, I make the meals
I use the essential spices and oils
Marjoram
Dill
Coriander, fennel
Garlic
Rosemary
The people I take care of

I caught cold
The man said
The man who talks about catching cold always looks pale
He says he can't hear because he's caught cold
He says he can't breathe through his nose because he's caught cold
He says he can't even understand the Japanese he overhears anymore
And so with all of the power in my body
I want to rain my breast milk and saliva
Upon his bad nose, his bad throat
To restore his organs to health
I want to rub and stroke him

In her sweet voice, my child too
Has a touch of cold
My youngest follows suit, her cold continues
Her habit of grasping my nipples also doesn't disappear
When grasped, my nipples hurt
They are withered, not a drop comes out
Grow old
We grow old
Menopause should have come

And so the many daughters whom I have born
Soak up the drips from my youngest daughter's nose
Wipe the diarrhea pouring from my youngest daughter's behind
Just like they were
Hundreds, thousands of mothers
Into this, they pour their accumulated desires
With her treatment, my youngest
Accepts the caresses of her older sisters
Her body becomes wrapped in song
She hears meaning in fragments
For such a long time, brown sugar, sweet, sweet, sweet, sweet
Meaning is in fragments without meaning
Sweet, sweet, sweet, coriander
Rosemary

My older sister told me she wanted to have her last child at
    thirty-nine
My older sister who grew up with me, five years my senior
That's what she thought when she saw that man
That man with the axe under his arm
That man with the axe under his arm and the nose ring
She schemed to have sex with him but
When she met him, her desire to give birth had faded
My older sister's girls are very big now
My younger sister's dream
Is to wander her whole life
To have children in distant lands with native men
To scatter children in those lands
Or so said my younger sister who grew up with me, two years
    my junior
Taking the children she wants
Leaving the children behind she doesn't
Wiping out the children she wants to kill
Marjoram

Rosemary
Fennel, coriander
We can still have more
We can still have more
If I gave birth again, I would live
With my older and younger sisters
If we wanted to touch each other erotically, we would do it
If we wanted to have sex, we'd go outside and do it
That's our promise
I'd eat with my sisters
My companions
Through speech and silence
We'd embrace
And listen to the sounds of
Each other's breath
Through the night

FROM *THE HEART SUTRA EXPLAINED* (2010)

THE HEART SUTRA

While looking freely and without effort at the world
While walking with people, searching for the path
In his spiritual quest to discern based on deep wisdom
Avalokiteshvara arrived at a certain thought.
The self is. All sorts of things are.
I sense that
I recognize that
I think about that
And it is the case that
In all things we discern
We are ourselves.
However, that means
Those things do *not exist*
I have understood that clearly
And I have escaped
All suffering and trouble.

Listen to this, Shariputra.

Being is not any different than *non-being*.
Non-being is not any different than *being*.

Things we think *are* really *are not*.
If we think of something as *non-being* that leads to *being*.

Sensing
Recognizing
Thinking
Discerning

Those things too are just as they are.
Listen to this, Shariputra.

All things that are, *are not*.
There is also no *living* or *dying*.
There is also no *dirty* or *clean*.
There is also no *increasing* or *decreasing*.

To put it another away
In *non-being*
There is no *being*.
There is also no *sensing*, no *recognizing*
Also no *thinking*, no *discerning*.
There are also no *eyes*, no *ears*, no *noses*, no *tongues*
Also no *bodies*, no *hearts*.
There are also no *colors*, no *shapes*, no *voices*, no *scents*, no *flavors*,
Also no *tangible things*, no *thought-provoking things*.
There is also no *world that can be seen with the eyes*.
There is also no *world that can be sensed by the heart*.
There are various things that arise from the workings of the human heart
Ranging from the world that can be seen with the eyes
To the world that can be sensed by the heart
But none of those exist,
Yet neither do their workings go away.

There is also no *suffering of not knowing*.
Nor does the *suffering of not knowing* go away.
There is also no *aging, dying, and suffering*
Nor does *aging, dying, and suffering* go away
Because people do not know
There are kinds of various kinds of suffering as we grow old and die
But none of those exist
Yet neither do those sufferings go away.

There is also no suffering in living.
There is also no confusion that creates suffering.
There is also no hope our suffering and our confusion
Will one day go away
Yet neither is there any effort to rid ourselves
Of suffering and confusion.

There is no *knowing*.
There is no *gaining*.

In other words, we cannot gain.
Therefore.
Those who search for the way
Follow this wisdom.
And then.
The things our hearts dwell upon go away.
All things we dwell upon go away.
Therefore.
Fear will go away.
All confusion will grow distant,
And the heart free of suffering will grow clear.
Present, past, future
All awakened ones always follow this wisdom
They have lived by it and will live by it.
And then.
It is clearly possible to awaken.
Therefore.
Know this wisdom that will carry you to the far shore.
This is a powerful incantation.
This is a powerful incantation that you will hear clearly.
This is the ultimate incantation.
This is an incantation that knows no equal.
All suffering will leave you immediately.
This is the truth. This is not a false claim.

Therefore.
I will tell you this wise incantation.
Here, I will tell you. This is how it goes.

Gyāte
Gyāte
Pāra gate
Pāra samgate
Bodhi svāhā

This has been the Heart Sutra.

NEW AND UNCOLLECTED POEMS

YAKISOBA

One day
At a supermarket where all the Japanese-Americans go
Someone called out and stopped me in my tracks
At the corner of the mall is an izakaya
Where they serve simmering kiriboshi daikon and hijiki
Next to that is a curry shop
Where they serve katsu curry and other things
Next to that is a Japanese-style cake shop
Where they serve strawberry shortcake
And in the fall, Mont Blanc
Next to that is the Japanese supermarket
An old woman works there in promotion
She yells in English with a strong accent
Probably in her late sixties, probably born and raised in Japan
Came here when she was young, probably lived here longer
Never to return
She uses only Japanese with her family
When she speaks in Japanese
Her children and grandchildren respond only in English
Today, just now, she yelled
And stopped a woman
"*Chotto okusan yottette*! Good sauce *ga* included *yo!*"
I was the one she stopped
My mind spun as I stopped
What the heck, who on earth
Is her yelling meant to stop?
What kind of person, what background, what gender, what station in life?
What does she want to say to the person she stops?
Aren't I the one?

The one who shares those things? Was I was the one who shared
The language, gender, age, station in life, interests, financial values
This lady was targeting? That was what was going through my mind
As I took a sample of her yakisoba
And tasted it with so much nostalgia
I took a bag of yakisoba, thinking *"Ara, kore wa* rather cheap *da wa ne!"*
Scrutinized it
And threw it into the shopping cart
All of the what
That are there?
Arigatō, she says
Iie, I say
Here is a woman
Who comes back alive, who comes back dead
Who connects with the next woman
With tens and hundreds and thousands of women
With generations, dozens of generations down the line

EELS AND CATFISH

A strange e-mail arrived
Hello to you
My name is Shimoda
And I'm a poet
Writing from Western Maine
I am wondering
If you might have any
Recommendations or suggestions
Of places to visit in or around Kumamoto
I responded. What do you want of me?
That was the first time I had received an e-mail, someone had approached me
Someone I didn't know, just because I live in Kumamoto
I imagined this Shimoda fellow was hoping I'd be nice
And say, well, why don't you stay with me?
But that is too presumptuous
Kumamoto summers are unbearably hot
Japanese houses are even hotter and more humid than the horrible weather outside
I hated the thought of taking in a complete stranger
But there was a day that I too had arrived like that
In an unfamiliar land
I ate the food people there gave me
I squandered the time people there provided
I felt like I had to repay my debt
So although terribly busy, I went into town in the horrific heat
And picked him up
But he was not one person but two
A young man and a young woman
I took them both out to eat some soba
As I read the menu out loud, I convinced them
This is the most *oosentikku*

Japaniizu fuudo in this town
Although that is not entirely true
We don't know, we'll just leave it up to you, they said
Not bothering to ask their likes and dislikes, I settled on sea eel tempura with soba
(The restaurant was in the Tokyo style and was really good
But we were in Kumamoto, and unfortunately it didn't have mustard-stuffed lotus roots
Or boiled green onions with sour miso, or raw horsemeat
The kinds of local delicacies one would expect in Kumamoto)
The two began to talk as we waited
We are looking for a place, a place called Nakanose
That was where my grandfather lived
We looked it up and found it
That place name is gone but
We think we'll go there anyway, take a bus
Today after we get done, they said
Their attitude, their wish to solve problems on their own
Gave me a good impression
Plus, they were both really young
And come to think of it, he was not just a poet
He was a Japanese-American
Hold on a minute, I said
I called Baba-san
Baba-san is a friend of mine
A long time ago when I lost everything
When I was left behind, defenseless in Kumamoto
He came up to me with a smile
And we have been doing things together ever since
As a civil servant, he has been transferred all over the prefecture
So he should know just about all the place names in Kumamoto
And as luck would have it, I got through to him in the middle of the day
I think you go along the Hamasen Bypass

And cross the Kase River, but hold on
I'll look it up, he told me
As they were eating their sea eel tempura and soba
And I was eating my junsai soba
Baba-san called back
I was right, go along the Hamasen Bypass, cross the Kase River, and it's there
He was right, the place name no longer exists
The name has been all but forgotten, it remains only in the name of a single restaurant
Tokunaga Eels, Nakanose Main Branch
Put the telephone number in your GPS and you'll be sure to get there
Then Baba-san specified
That place is in Catfish
And so we went
Leaving town, even after leaving town
There were rows upon rows of dull city streets
Then suddenly our path went down a narrow lane with nothing on it
Then the narrow lane gave way to a broad street
That was the Hamasen Bypass
Lined with boring city buildings
Rows of convenience stores and family restaurants
Rows of chain stores just like you might find anywhere
Rows of gaudy signs
Pachinko parlors raising a racket
Suddenly a large mall appeared
The parking lot stretching on endlessly
We crossed the bridge across the Kase River
At the foot of the bridge was a restaurant that specialized in eel
The aroma of barbequed eel filled the air
Beyond the restaurant was nothing but rice paddies
I stopped the car at the embankment and he walked around
Smoke was coming out of the eel restaurant
The air was full of a delicious scent

Neither he nor his wife knew
That scent came from the barbequed eels
That the scent alone makes you want to eat and eat
When his grandfather was nine
He set out alone for America
His family had already gone, the reason
He was left behind alone was because he was sick
After he recovered, the nine year-old boy
Went alone from Kumamoto to Oita, then set sail for Yokohama
Changed boats in Yokohama, then arrived in San Francisco
All alone
In the rice paddies across the way was a cemetery
Can we go in there?
He asked hesitantly
Sure, let's do it
I told him we could take the car and go over there
The narrow farming road went on and on
The water flowed alongside unbroken
There was a board forming a bridge from the road to the cemetery
There were more than ten gravestones
And there I found it, a gravestone marked Shimoda, the same name
It must be a relative, a direct one or not, I could not be sure
But looking at the wide-open landscape around the rice paddies
I could imagine how stubborn society must be
I could imagine his had not been the main branch but an offshoot
    of the family
A branch family goes out into the world, it splits off
And the descendant of that family
Like a nine year-old boy
Crosses the Pacific, goes from Yokohama to Oita, then arrives in
    Kumamoto
All alone
And stands face to face
With the grave where generations of the Shimoda family are buried

Next to that
Is the grave of Shimoda Takayuki
An army sergeant who died in the 1940s
Killed on the battlefield in his early twenties
(I took a photo of it on my cell phone, just now as I searched for it
A picture of my dead aunt's face suddenly came up on the screen
My aunt who died just recently, I did not go to the funeral
My cousin sent it, I wanted to erase it, but I could not bring myself to do it
I keep my aunt, her dead face, her corpse in my cell phone)
On the far side of the road was Catfish
The name of the place was written clear as day on the telephone pole
   Catfish, Kashima Town, Mashiki County
In ancient times, a caldera formed in Aso and collected lots of water
A big, big lake formed there, and a big, big catfish lived inside
The god Takeiwatatsu-no-mikoto came and ruled over the area
He kicked the side of the lake with his feet
The water overflowed and ran out, running, running, running all over the place
It ran and ran
It swallowed everything up
Everything perished
The native catfish was alive though
Takeiwatatsu-no-mikoto killed it by cutting it up
He chopped it up
Into little pieces
The place was covered in blood, but the water washed it away
A piece of the catfish was washed to this distant place
So this place is called Catfish
They call it that even now
A tiny, mud-colored frog jumped
From the top of the plank bridge down below
Tiny, mud-colored frogs jumped in the muddy water
The water had retreated but the trees and grasses

And vines had grown, covering traces of blood
Covering the slaughter
A blue heron walked slowly in the green rice paddy
When I started the car
The Japanese-American turned
Looked over his shoulder
And waved in the direction of his own past

ANPANMAN AND JOHNNIES

The Japanese School is not
Supported by the Ministry of Education
The Japanese in the name does not mean
Japanese people but Japanese language
Even so, everyone is taught to call it
Nihonjin gakkō—Japanese peoples' school
It takes place here every Friday night
It is a place where Japanese people that either
Do not want to go home or who cannot go home
Give language to their Nikkei children
Japanese Songs
Delicious things
The seasons that ordinarily would be going by
What they think is amusing, what they think is hateful
In each nursery school classroom
The Nikkei children watch Anpanman
Their hair is brown, eyes are round
An old lady passing by shouts out
She came from Japan as a bride generations before
Well, they all look so much alike!
You can hardly tell
Which child belongs to whom!
To tell the truth, all of the children's Japanese-born parents
Thought exactly the same thing but
They held back from saying it aloud
As if they had come up against some code
As if it would be discriminatory
As if everyone wanted to think of them as a group
To give the phenomenon a name, as if they were related
As if they were all suffering from some disease not afflicting
    the parents
A disease

Perhaps they were diseased, as proof
Only English comes out when they open their mouths
Even the children that speak Japanese so well at home
Develop mysterious inflections develop in their Japanese on the way here
I am not a native speaker of this language
It doesn't affect me, leave me alone, they say
It is the intonation of confirmation
They do not speak the heavily accented English of their mothers
As if in confirmation
The pimple-faced Nikkei faces in middle-school class
Sing their Johnnies songs

MOTHER DIES

One day, I drive an hour and a half to the Japanese consulate
In order to verify
That I am myself
Mother had died
I need to close, to close mother's account
There is something in it, a paltry amount
But if the account comes of age without me doing certain procedures
I cannot close it, cannot close that account
I fill out documents upon documents
At the bank, the elderly man tells me
To collect documents upon documents
In order to verify
My mother was my mother
My father was my father
I am myself
I did not want to give in to the tedium
Money is still valuable, even in paltry sums, so I kept at it
It dawned on me there was one account, one without a bankbook
Mother made it, father didn't know about it
All sorts of
Situations and feelings and
Tensions and disappointments
Come leaking out and filled my ears
The bank teller continues, the balance is 518 yen
And if there is no bankbook, it must be treated as lost
And that requires more documents upon documents, he tells me
Let's forget it
I gently suggest but he cannot let it go
I fill out even more
Documents and documents
I collect documents upon documents
A document verifying

My mother is my mother
A document verifying
My mother was born as this person
A document verifying
She was always my mother
Even though she changed names and addresses again and again
A document that we could not verify
My mother was my mother
(The entire city went up in flames in the Great Tokyo Air Raid)
A document that I, the one filling out the papers, am my father's proxy
Even though the money would go into my father's account
A document verifying
I am my father's daughter
A document verifying
My father has always been my father from the start
A document verifying
My father continues to be my father even now
Then once we had collected every document imaginable
I have to verify
That I am me
So far, those are problems anyone might face, anyone from Japan
The situation is so tedious that sometimes people
Live a decade or two beyond one hundred
However
I cannot verify who I am
I am a non-resident
I do not have a certificate verifying my name stamp
I do not have a certificate verifying my residence or granting health insurance
The bank teller becomes flustered
If you cannot verify yourself, we cannot complete the procedure
But he cannot forget either
It was the first time a non-resident had come to talk to him

I was not trying to commit fraud, cover something up, or rob a corpse
The situation is just what it is
I was just trying to let the bank know
What is going on
That was when the boss stepped in and spoke
Go back home to where you live and go to the Japanese consulate
Get the signature verification forms and come back
Signature verification—shomei shōmei in Japanese
Sounds strange, but that is the only way you can publically
Verify you are you, he said
So when I come to the window at the consulate
That is something they are used to
I fill out the application and hand it over with my passport
That's when I think, I might as well ask for it too, a certificate to vote as a non-resident
I have always wanted that, wanted to get one
I could participate in Japanese politics if I had one
I had been thinking about that, wanting to get one
But the consulate is so far and such a hassle so I had not bothered
And in the end so just went on living
Ten years without political participation
Dawdling my time away, living like grass without roots
Once I talked about this with Tawada-san in Germany
Of course I have it, she said
And so I reproached myself
Now I will be able to get it, without any trouble
Because I am here
I have come to the consulate
So I fill out, fill out forms
I hand it over, hand over my passport
I pay, pay the service fee
Several days later, it comes, I get it
It comes to me by mail, it reaches me
Very official, very Japanese

Thick paper with a watermark, greenish blue and brownish yellow
That is when it becomes clear
In Japan, there is nothing that exists clearly
Even in elections, everyone dawdles through
I had thought my own existence was certain
But now I understand
Things are indeterminate, colors and shapes
Things are indeterminate, even sounds
Is it an /l/ or an /r/?
It all makes sense now
It is not just a problem with me but with all Nikkeijin
Whether we have the right to vote or not
Is it an /ɪˈlɛk ʃən/ or an /ɪˈrɛk ʃən/?
Each time we Nikkeijin go to an election
Must we get our citizenship to have the right to vote
Or should we Nikkeijin just have an erection instead?
(I wish I could just have an erection
But there are many things I cannot do because I am a Nikkeijin)
And we have lived such indeterminate lives

COOKING, WRITING POETRY

A huge earthquake, a huge tsunami
People die and just moments later
There's the nuclear meltdown
Drawn-out fear assaults us
Each time I go to Tokyo
It is darker
Hot and humid there
It stings
In Tokyo
Everyone was afraid
Everybody was angry

Neko has been my close friend for thirty years
Cooking is her profession
I had a dream, she said
We were coming home after going to see the giant sequoias
I was driving
She was nodding off next to me but then suddenly woke
And began saying, when I was young
I had a dream
I had a baby
The baby was with me
But I couldn't breastfeed it
The baby was dying right before my eyes
But I couldn't breastfeed it
That was how the dream went
Maybe
That was from a past life
And that karma
Is the reason I now cook
Morning and night like this
Feeding the children

Of other people

Now she is doing something
She calls the "Nicomaru Cookie" project
First she called the young women in Tokyo
In Tokyo all alone
All alone and anxious
And unable to stand it any longer
All of them in Tokyo
All of them made cookies
And sold them
And sent the proceeds to the disaster zone
And then she changed gears and brought to Tokyo
The food the people in the disaster zone had made
And sold it in the city
She worked her fingers to the bone
And hired some staff
And went to the disaster zone
And cooked
She went into town
And started collecting signatures for an anti-nuclear petition
She made dozens of dishes each day
Even though she had her parents to care for
Even though she was working
Her fingers to the bone
She moves around, in the crisis
The only thing she knew to do
Was to cook like that
The only thing she could do
She couldn't help but cook
And work her fingers to the bone
And I watched her do it
Powerless, useless
There is an expression

Take the dirt from under someone's nails
Boil it and make it into tea
It means to admire someone so much
You would do those things
I asked her for some and she gave it to me
When I made it into tea
It was sour and sweet

Poets wrote poetry
The thoughts rained down continuously
Drenching us to the bone
So many poems were written
Like Kaneko Misuzu
Even easier to understand than Kaneko Misuzu
Unsightly poems
Boring poems
But still they were read
They say people read them and wept
I heard lots of stories like that
Don't cry
Don't write
Don't miss out
From that perspective
They cannot say no
The poets
Who can do nothing but write
Cannot say no to writing
They cannot relate except
Through writing
They must not
Say no
They must not
Fail to be read

Yesterday Jeffrey
Asked me to help him with a translation
Some American poet had written a poem about the disaster
I tried reading it, but it was a complete cliché
That guy
Had not even been to Japan
He wrote the poem looking at pictures
Complete cliché
But that guy had seen pictures of the disaster
He saw them
And his heart was moved
So he had no choice but write
The clichés he tried to convey
In a clichéd way ended up clichés
But still it was a good poem

I could not write
After all, the places I live
Are in California and Kumamoto
There was no shaking
The radioactivity didn't reach us
I didn't want to write
I couldn't write
A clichéd poem
Like that guy in America
I could not do a thing
The only thing I did
Was to translate and read out loud the second part of
An Account of My Ten-Square Foot Hut
I took that old text that depicted so vividly
The earthquakes
The tsunamis
Nine hundred years ago
Put it into my own voice

And sent out my voice like this
> *Around the same time, we suffered another terrible earthquake*
> *Unparalleled in its force*
> *The mountains collapsed, the rivers were buried*
> *The sea crashed in, inundating the land*
> *The earth broke, water bubbled up*
> *The boulders split and tumbled into the valleys*
> *The boats plying the water were tossed by the waves*
> *The horses traveling the roads were unable to keep their footing*
> *In one area of the capital, no place, no building*
> *Escaped unscathed, they collapsed or leaned to the side*
> *Dust and ashes and smoke billowed up*
> *Both the sound of the moving earth and the collapsing houses*
> *Were just like peals of thunder*
> *Those who were inside were crushed on the spot*
> *Those who ran were swallowed up by the cracks in the earth…*
> *The worst of the shaking continued for a while then stopped*
> *The aftershocks continued for some time*
> *Everyday, twenty, thirty times a day*
> *There were aftershocks large enough to terrify us ordinarily*
> *Ten days went by, twenty days went by, receeding into the past*
> *There were four or five aftershocks per day, then two or three*
> *Then every other day, then two or three days in between*
> *The aftershocks continued for three months*

This way
The earthquake
The tsunami
Crept into my body (just a little)

And then I read the Buddhist classics
For instance, the Lotus Sutra, *I am always*
Asking myself, how can I
Share the truth with living beings
Share the Buddha's teachings

Or the Amida Sutra, *All who want*
To be born in the land of happiness
Or all who will one day request that
Or who are requesting that right now
They will all awake to the truth, they will not return
To the confusion
Or the Nirvana Sutra, *Each and every living being*
Has the heart of the Buddha
That's right, it was Mahayana Buddhism
That said so clearly to the Buddhists of the time
During an era when they were reading for all they were worth
Not sure if they understood or not
But obsessed with grasping the truth
You are wrong
Entirely wrong
First you help people
That is what it is to be a bodhisattva
All I've experienced is an earthquake and tsunami nine hundred years ago
But if I were to put into my own words
And deliver a message to
This wounded
Damaged
Frightened
Trembling society
That's no doubt what it would be
That would be best
Or
So I hope
If not then
I would not even know
Which direction to turn

HIRATA TOSHIKO

FROM *TERMINAL* (1997)

GREETINGS ARE IMPORTANT

When you're going to cross a bridge
Use the greeting "Please let me pass"
If you don't, the bridge will break in two
As you make it halfway across

When you're going to climb into a car
Use the greeting "Please let me in"
If you don't, the tires will deflate
As you as you sit in the seat

When you're about to swim in a pool
Use the greeting "Please let me swim here"
If you don't, the pool will turn to sand
As you dip in your feet

When you're about to wipe your face
Use the greeting "Please let me wipe with you"
If you don't, the towel will feel pain
As you apply it to your face

When you're about to lie in bed
Use the greeting "Please let me sleep here"
If you don't, the bed will become a casket
As you fall fast asleep

MY FUN FAMILY

The crows of August
Have been staring at us
From early morning onward so
Father can't go work at the government bureau
Mother can't go negotiate with the insurance
Daughter can't go work at the design office
Son can't go teach social studies

The crows of August
Have been staring at us
Even in the afternoon so
Father can't go to his dance lessons
Mother can't go meet her tennis coach
Daughter can't go scuba diving
Son swings an invisible bat in the living room

The crows of August
Have been starting at us
Even after night has fallen
Father can't go burn down the warehouse
Mother can't go swindle her sweetheart
Daughter can't go hijack a taxi
Son can't go kidnap the children

COMPLAINTS FROM THE INHABITANT

Who's climbing the apartment wall?
Walls aren't there for climbing
They're there for graffiti

Who's speaking on the apartment roof?
Roofs aren't there for speaking
They're there for dancing down the rain

Who's polishing the apartment windows?
Windows aren't there for polishing
They're there for breaking gleefully

Who's crying under the floorboards?
The space beneath isn't there for crying
It's for thieves to hide and drink their booze

Who's falling down the stairs?
The stairs aren't there for falling
They're there for hanging lines of squid to dry

Who's knocking at the door?
The door isn't there for knocking
It's there, rising so precipitously
To separate me from you

WEIRD

Doesn't that family seem a little weird?
The TV antenna lies there where it has fallen
The nameplate by their front door is cheap wood
They only do their laundry once a month
They've got a big Buddha in their yard
(I saw this peeking through the hedge)

Doesn't that family seem a little weird?
The husband leads cows home at night
The wife goes out in the morning to dance
The children go to school buck-naked
They're growing mushrooms in the tatami
(I saw this peeking through the bathroom window)

Doesn't that family seem a little weird?
The husband manufactures missiles
The wife polishes the knives
The children read books about adult diseases
They chill their socks in the refrigerator
They eat their meals underneath the table
(I noticed this peeking from the kitchen)

Doesn't that family seem a little weird?
It's been a whole year since they've moved here
They don't bring year-end gifts
They don't come talk things over
They travel as a family over New Year's
They're cooking up some kind of plan
(I heard this crawling beneath their floorboards)

P-E-O-P-L-E

Please let me hear your voice
Please listen to my voice

Please draw a window you like
Please let me paint the color I like

Please lend me your lake
Feel free to climb my mountain

Please show me your collarbone
Let's exchange one of yours for mine

Please show me your line of fortune
I'll give you part of my life line

Please let me touch your narrative
Please embrace my history

Please show me your wounds
Please take a look at my scars

Please show me what you look like in tears
I also cry so I'd like you by my side

Please draw me a map
Of the town where you were born
Once day I'd like to go there with you

Please show me your shadow
Let's line yours up with mine
No doubt the two will look a lot alike

Please tell me your name
Please ask me my name as well

THE CAT STAYS EVEN AFTER IT'S GONE, AND I CAST MY SUSPICIONS ON IT

This cat, why does he smile now?
While alive, he was so abrupt
Never smiled even once
Now that he's a photograph
He shows me his hairy grin

This cat, why does he meow now?
While alive, he was so silent
Never even cried out once
Now that he's a photograph
He meows with a voice like static

This cat, why does he walk now?
While alive, he was so indolent
Never even took a single step
Now that he's a photograph
He steps out of the picture for a walk

This cat, why does he eat now?
While alive, he was so set against food
Never even ate a thing
Now that he's a photograph
He eats tomorrow's dinner too

CAN'T GET THROUGH

Are you angry about something?

Or maybe you are sick
Or away on a trip
Or maybe even incarcerated
Or bound arm and foot
Or sometimes the phone breaks
Or maybe you've been relaxing in the bath
Or been asleep this whole time
If not, then you must
Have forgotten about me
Long ago

But

Was there ever anyone there?
I am a secret, living in this world
If anyone calls me
It is my mother
Or the landlord
Or a detective
Or a prank call
Or someone selling something
Or maybe even me
Calling from some day far away

THE NEXT DAY

Yesterday
Someone was weeping here at this house
The solemn gate, usually
Shut so tight, was open
And the sobbing seeped outside
Many people hung their heads
And entered the gate one after another
A group of them stood by the road
And smoked cigarettes
And whispered in small voices
Ordinarily
There's not a sign of anyone
This manor is like a shut-down school
But with a single sadness
It was as full as a school entrance ceremony
Today
I pass by again
The gate is shut tighter than ever
The voices full of heightened emotion
Are nowhere to be heard
Not even if you prick up your ears
Neither the shadows nor the warmth
Of the gathered people remain on the road
As one night dawns, the warmth retreats
And the world is quiet as ever

LOTS OF VISITORS

Everyone comes to see the divorced
I don't think a divorced woman is all that rare these days
But they say they don't mind returning for another look
The diplomat from the insurance company
Reproaches me for not having divorce insurance
And leaves me some literature
The babysitter
Tells me I must be sad living alone
And leaves me a baby no one needed
The mystery fan
Checks behind the dresser, peeks in the attic
And furtively leaves me the manual *How to Commit the Perfect Crime*
The volunteer
Expertly tells the tales of other people's divorces
Then tells me
She's got to go visit someone on her deathbed
And promptly takes her leave
The nameplate maker
Goes home without leaving anything, or so I thought
Later, on the other side of the door
I found a finely crafted nameplate that says,
The divorced woman lives here.

THE VACANT SEAT

He left his seat
To take a seat in another chair
In another room
With another someone
He forgot the seat on purpose
He should have taken care
Of his seat through to the end
I persuade the abandoned chair
To go chase after him
But it pretends not to hear
It cannot leave the table
A vacant seat is an eyesore
So I carry it to the trash
But each time I do
It rushes briskly back
(Its four legs make it fast)
If I put it in water, it won't dissolve
If I step upon it, it won't break
If I hang it out in the sun, maybe
It'll turn into a four-legged beast
So I hang it out on the balcony
But the chair stays a chair
The two words *vacant seat* bleed
And wait for someone's behind

UPSTANDING CREATURES

When it grows light
The first thing they do is make noise
After all, even birds are upstanding creatures
When tempted with toys
The first thing they do is follow
After all, even school kids are upstanding creatures
When wearing a suit
The first thing they do is go out
After all, even office workers are upstanding creatures
When cars get near
The first thing they do is turn red
After all, even traffic lights are upstanding creatures
When they have the resolve
The first thing they do is break in
After all, even thieves are upstanding creatures
When their life is over
The first thing they do is die
After all, even stray cats are upstanding creatures

(I'm the guy who turned the page on that world
And decided to try to get some sleep)
I don't get hungry when I hear the clock chime
I don't open my eyes even when I get enough sleep
When I lie down, I hear things clearly
Even the footsteps of people far away
Strike my ears like raindrops)

When a mountain is nearby
The first thing they do is climb
After all, even mountaineers are upstanding creatures
When the birds make noise
The first thing it does is show its face

After all, even the sun is an upstanding creature
When today ends
It will come back again
After all, I'm a fairly upstanding creature too

MAKING UP MY MIND

I'll call at 9 a.m.
To say something's come up and
I have to cancel our plans today
But at 9 a.m. you'll still be asleep

I'll call at 10 a.m.
That's because a woman
Gave birth to a baby
That didn't look like its father
That didn't even look human
But at 10 a.m. is when you gargle

I'll call at 11 a.m.
The man went pale then flushed red
He grabbed the mother by the hair
And banged her repeatedly against the wall
But 11 a.m. is your silent time

I'll call at 12 noon
The man wouldn't settle down
Instead he grabbed the baby by the head
And tossed it out the window
But 12 noon is when you eat your cake

I'll call at 1 p.m.
The man wouldn't settle down
Instead he ran to the stable
And killed the cows and pigs
But 1 p.m. is when you paint

I'll call at 2 p.m.
The man still wouldn't settle down

Instead he got an axe out of the barn
And smashed the bed and chest of drawers
But 2 p.m. is when you read your biographies

I'll call at 3 p.m.
The man still wouldn't settle down
Instead he flew into the house across the street
And kicked their newborn pup
But 3 p.m. is when you do your exercises

I'll call at 4 p.m.
The dog-owner wouldn't settle down
Instead he kicked the man back of course
And everyone applauded
But 4 p.m. is when you peel your peaches

I'll call at 5 p.m.
The man still, still wouldn't settle down
Instead he rushed home at top speed
And pulled out his rifle
But 5 p.m. is when you play your keyboard

I'll call at 6 p.m.
The man tried to shoot the dog-owner
But the puppy bit him
And everyone applauded again
But 6 p.m. is when you take your swim

I'll call at 7 p.m.
The man dejectedly left
Returned home and had a beer
And the once dead baby
Began to breathe again
But 7 p.m. is when you tend the garden

I'll call at 8 p.m.
The resurrected baby now looked just like dad
No one had any doubt that it was his
The man's mistake had been cleared up
But now it was the baby who wouldn't settle down
But 8 p.m. is when you sit by the fireplace

I'll call at 9 p.m.
The mother immediately flew at the man
Hoping to dispel her grief
A nearby candle fell to the floor
And lit the hem of the curtains
But 9 p.m. is when you eat your beans

I'll call at 10 p.m.
The couple didn't notice the fire
And were having an intimate scuffle
When the flames licked upward
Moving next door like a rumor
But 10 p.m. is when you breathe

I'll call at 11 p.m.
My house was next door
It was a matter of time before it burned
That's the reason
I want to cancel our plans
But 11 p.m. is when you take your walk

I'll call tomorrow
To say something came up and
I had to cancel our plans yesterday afternoon
I'll be sure to call tomorrow

MAN WITHOUT ARMS

A man was standing there without arms
He and I faced each other across the crosswalk
Suspended between us like a rope bridge
The man didn't have either of his arms
He walked this way when the light turned green
I looked at my shoes as I walked
Pretending to be worried
I walked by him
Once I had reached the other side
Once I had cut the bridge down, I turned to look
I looked at the man's old jacket
I watched as the two empty sleeves
Fluttered in the wind

I was the one who cut off his arms
I amputated them with a saw
Like getting rid of two extra branches
So he couldn't hold the steering wheel
So he couldn't play the keyboard
So he couldn't open the door and go
So he couldn't go where she was
So he couldn't grab her breast
So he couldn't strangle her
I sawed with all my might
I did it well, considering it was my first time
Even he complimented me on my skill
The body of the armless man
Was as clean as a tree in winter
But

Arms grow back over and over again
When he reaches her room

The two empty sleeves of his jacket
Will have filled out like branches
Even when I split him clean in two
The arms keep growing back over and over again

FROM *TREASURES* (2007)

WE MAKE IT A POINT TO WASH OUR HANDS

We wash our hands when we've come in from outside
We wash our hands when we've been inside all day

We wash our hands after we wash the meat
We wash our hands after we wash the tea

We wash our hands before we wash our hair
We wash our hands before we wash our hands

We wash our hands (in the wind) when the wind blows
We wash our hands (in the rain) when the rain falls

We wash our hands before meeting people
We wash our hands after meeting people

We wash our hands in the flames of candles
We wash our hands in the darkness after blowing them out

We wash our hands, wetting our cuffs
We wash our hands, caring little our hands will get wet

We wash our hands before going to sleep at night
We wash our hands once again in our dreams

We wash our hands before we remember someone
We wash our hands after we have remembered someone
And then immediately we forget them once again

What comes from the faucet is water that is scalding hot
Or water that is much too cold

We either get burn blisters
Or frostbite
We wash our hands not caring about that

We wash our hands to calm our Lines of Heart
We wash our hands to disrupt our Lines of Fate

We wash our hands to confirm our existence
We wash our hands to wipe our existence out

CAMERA

You take my sweet sleeping face
You take my innocent smile
You take my large breasts
Even though I asked you not to

You take the mole on my shoulder
You take the blouse I have taken off
You take my dirty room
Even though I asked you not to

You take me when I am angry
You take me when I get hit
You take me when I get kicked across the room
Even though I do not know you have done it

You take my house when it is burning
You take my younger brother when he is falling
You take my younger sister when she is collapsing
You take my older brother when he burns to death
You take my older sister when she kills herself
You take my mother as she is weeping
Is that because I didn't tell you not to take them?

You take the dry skin on my arms and legs
You take my swollen face
You take my crooked spine
You take my hair that has fallen out
I no longer have the strength to tell you no

This one's no good, this one's good
This one's no good, this one's good
As you look at the monitor

You choose the photos
The versions of me that survive
The versions of me that are erased
(The versions of me that survive
(The versions of me that are erased
Even if you erase me
It doesn't mean you didn't take me
(Even if you erase me
(It doesn't mean you didn't take me
You took me
And erased me
(You took me
(And erased me
You took lots of me
You erased lots of me
More of me than what you took
Disappeared with the work of a single finger

VAN GOGH'S *BEDROOM* AS I SEE IT

There are two chairs in this room
Both are simple, unsophisticated chairs
Their gender is unclear
Their age also unclear
Both of them are simple but
The chair on the left is a little more grown up
Than the one on the right
Maybe it is the older brother
And the one on the left the younger sister

There is a table between the chairs
The table wears a worn out expression
The chairs and table are not lovers
Their relationship is that of parent and child
The table is mother to the chairs

What stands out most is the bed
Which takes up nearly half the room
The bed's volume is greater than that
Of the table and both chairs put together
Still, the bed is not especially ashamed
About what a giant it is

The chair and table are standing
But the bed is lying down
It is not doing so well these days
"Get better, daddy"
"Get better, darling"
The wife and her two children
Watch over it with worried expressions

The husband doesn't have much longer
The blood that has drained from him
Has stained the floor an ominous color
The wife holds a pitcher and cup
Ready to carry water to her dying husband

The large piece of cloth hanging on the wall
Is to shroud the father's corpse when he dies
The older brother has already secretly decided
That will be his job when the time comes

Unaware of what is happening
His little sister crowds close to her father
But does not utter a word

The artist who painted this
Shot himself in a wheat field at the end of his life
The artist who painted this
Was not blessed with family while he was alive

The color of the bed in the room
So strongly resembles the color of wheat
While the walls of the room
So strongly resemble the color of the sky
Stretching over the field of wheat

LEMONS

Why does *lemon* レモン become *lemon* 檸檬
When you write it in characters?
It was a mystery to me for ages
I couldn't understand
How two characters
Could take the place of three

Looking it up, I found a superficial answer
Some foreigner said "lémən"
To someone who misheard "reimou"
And thus the characters were assigned

We can't laugh at the person who misheard
When one first encounters
Words from other countries
Confusion usually follows

They say when Kajii Motojirō wrote "The Lemon"
He called it レモン in the first draft
But later changed the title to 檸檬
I don't know if there was a first draft or not
But Takamura Kōtarō titled his *Lemon Elegies* with the word レモン
Still, when I think of the latter half of his wife Chieko's life
The oppressiveness of the characters 檸檬
Seem more appropriate
Than the brightness of レモン

In his "Topaz Fragrance," he colors
Her suffering leading to madness
Her madness leading to death
With a beautiful hue
But that has a whiff of falsehood to me

After five months, Kōtarō sent his wife
Some lemons as a get-well gift
Her condition quickly worsened that night
And her life ended at age fifty-two
But do people's deaths
Really come so conveniently
Like the stuff of poetry?

James-zaka Hospital, the psychiatric ward in southern Shinagawa
Where Chieko spent three years and nine months, is long gone
All that remains is a blackened stele carved with *Lemon Elegies*
One day when I visited, there was an offering
A small basket with several lemons
How long had they been there?
All the lemons were dry and ugly
More like lemons 檸檬
Standing in for lemons レモン
And it struck me that those horrifying fruits
Were more appropriate for poor Chieko
If Kōtarō were still alive
Probably he would have used his huge, powerful hands
To sweep away those monsters
Which had lost all freshness and life

WATER

At a public symposium
Called "Crime, Punishment, and Me"
Three foreigners take to the podium

Seated in the middle, Raskolnikov
Has been arguing vociferously
All by himself since the very start
He speaks in a foreign language
So I cannot understand
I only follow when he gets tongue-tied
He gestures, "Excuse me a second"
Gulps down a glass of water
Then once again begins
His passionate diatribe

Seated to the right is Porfiry
Who listens silently until partway through
When he cocks his head hard to the side
Tilts his head to the side three times
Gulps down two glasses of water
Then interrupts Raskolnikov and starts to speak
In a low, calm voice

It turns out to be true
Words are made of water
Words are born of water
Seated on the left is Marmeladov
Who spits at his water often, not saying a thing
The hand holding his cup is trembling
He must be fairly nervous
Before long, the jug with the water is empty
He gestures, "Excuse me a second"

Stands up and runs to the restroom
Never to return

It turns out to be true
Transform the water you drink into words
If you don't, you'll have to run to the restroom
Are water and words both forms of punishment?

The guests in their seats
Quietly watch the symposium develop
No one gives them water so
No words come forth
With worried expressions
Sonya, Dunya, and Razumikhin
All merely watch

Clear water
Cloudy water
Cracked water
Red water
Water patrols the insides of our bodies and searches out words
And as punishment for drinking water
Words make us suffer as we vomit them out

TREASURE

The most beautiful word in the world is Concertgebouw

Four years ago in Amsterdam
Shaken by the afternoon train
I spied a large building before us
What's that? I asked
The Concertgebouw, you answered

Concertgebouw
At the time I didn't know
What that meant
But when you whispered the word
Your voice was so lovely
That I have treasured it ever since

Until then I had never heard
Anyone utter that word
Nor have I since
The only time you whispered it
Was on that day
A word heard only once
That I alone heard
Your
Soft
Voice
That day

Writing it down like this
My treasure quickly loses its luster
Becoming less than a discarded cicada husk
I revealed this secret
To get rid of something dear

To forget both
You and that word

Goodbye
My Concertgebouw
My heart will never again beat quickly for you
One has to dispose of what is precious
Over and over again

Even the sweet dew of separation
Grows thin as I write about it here
I am not the least bit hurt
And that, I think, is
The most unfortunate part

DISTANT SKY

In those days, there were still staircases
Climb them and you would reach high places
There were potted plants at the top of the stairs
And inside the pots, dark, dry earth
There were still fountains in the plazas
Sitting around that, people with nothing to do

In those days, there was an untrained but skilled doctor
Who gave us effective shots in the arm
Afterwards, we would always get fevers
But when they went down, the sickness went away too
There were still keyholes in the doors
Where the keys would work without sleep

In those days, I was alive
And that person was not dead
Touch him, and his lips were cold
And his gaze was even colder

There was a fence around the town
And beyond that, an unknown sky
It was easy to cross the fence
But impossible to go more than ten steps

MORNING ILLUSIONS

Why is it we want to open so many things
When we wake up in the morning?
Open the curtains, open the windows
Open the white refrigerator door
Open the lid to the tomato juice
Open our mouths to drink
Is it honeybees (蜜蜂) or honey (蜂蜜) we spread on our bread?
Still unsure, I put a slice in the toaster
Open the door to get the newspaper
When I was a girl, there was a calendar
From the saké shop on a pillar at home
I didn't really understand what it said
Things like *tsuchinoe* (つちのえ) and *shakkō* (赤口)
In small letters beneath the dates
Things other than dates and days of the week
Inhabited our calendar so each morning
I got nervous as I tore off another of its thin pages

The newspaper is clearer than the calendar
The word *truth* (真相) is clearly visible
I draw close wondering which truth they mean
When I realize I misread the word *prime minister* (首相)
The magazine *Rumored Truths* (噂の真相) has stopped publishing
But where is the rumored prime minister (噂の首相) right now?

Sometimes people call the prime minister *sōsai* (総裁) or "president"
But this reminds me of the word *sōsai* (相殺) or "cancel out"
This word does not always mean "kill each other" (殺し合い)
As the characters might imply
But even so, it sends a chill up my spine

Looking at it with sleepy eyes
My calendar looks more like a calendar
Each morning as I tear out my eyes
The world looks like a new place

FROM *THE FREEDOM OF THE JOKE* (2015)

BEAUTIFUL STAPLES

Some of the documents that came today
Were fastened with beautiful staples
The color of dayflowers
For me who had known nothing but gray staples
Their color was fresh and new
Their elegant color made my heart
As heavy as an overcast sky
Just a little lighter

The purpose of staples is to fasten
No need to worry about their color
But somewhere someone dyed them that lovely hue
Somewhere someone chose those staples
And one of them
Made the journey to me
I feel as if I have joined hands
With those strangers
Through a dayflower

It is not just flowers
That calm human hearts
Even small, dangerous things
That cut a finger in a moment of carelessness
Can set our hearts at play
When the sky runs with sunrise or sunset
When the sky is dyed any color but blue
We are filled and stand transfixed

AT SOME POINT THINGS GET ROUGH

Emotions are either straight or curved lines
Sometimes digressions or dashes
The three-dot ellipsis … shows
Lingering sensation, silence, and summarization
Just these three infants
Carrying such heavy weight……
……………………………
Sorry to have ever been born…
I never want to see you again…
A line of dots hinting along those lines
I am always tracing a line parallel to yours
After nine instances of the ellipsis
Is Urashima Tarō, stabbed in the back……
Throw either a fastball or a curve and still
The ball flies high and falls back to the ground

DO NOT TREMBLE

It trembles
It is trembling again today
I did not know that the earth
Is an unruly cradle
A cruel cradle that lets
Neither adult nor child sleep

It is March, it is spring
It should be a gentle season of vernal sleep
When one sleeps so deeply there is no dawn
But spring this year
Shakes us to keep us
From falling asleep

Earth, it is enough
For you simply to
Keep spinning happily
Leave the trembling
To windblown flowers and
Laundry hanging in the year
You should simply spin
Innocently

Those forces that shake the earth
May you turn to bubbles and disappear
Do not tremble
Do not trem
Do not tre
Do not
Not
No!

COLD SPRING

I grind the beans
Pour in the hot water little by little
And make two cups of coffee
One for me
The other for someone no longer here

You were susceptible to cold
I should have wrapped a scarf around you
I should have given you gloves
But I sent you off empty-handed
The too-cold water boils
With flames of regret

Life is hard, death is easy
Does it help to think that way?
In the bright light and sweet wind
I pretend not to know the answer

Flowers bloom, birds sing
Spring comes without a certain someone
Fragments of feeling muttered to myself
Spill over, more than I can count

I will keep the water always at a boil
So that those who are cold may warm themselves
So that I can make coffee at a moment's notice
Even on the days no one will return

ARAI TAKAKO

FROM *SOUL DANCE* (2007)

GIVE US MORNING

Morning is the time we count the dead
In the newspapers, in the hospitals, on the roads, on the seashores
In the rubble that was once our homes
Possess us all the more, Amenouzume-san
The morning is still not enough

We still cannot count them all
We still cannot carry them all
Dance more for us, Amenouzume-san
Put a green twig in your hair
And call out to them
Give the dead
To morning
Possess them, call out to them

> *It's me, the girl floating here this whole time*
> *It's me, Mama's boy crouched down*
> *It's me, the boy with the right arm wrenched off*
> *I want to see you again, I want to see you again*
> *A bullet to the temple*
> *I scratch my throat, it hurts*
> *Now I'm sinking as far as I can go*
> *Why? Why was I the boy*
> *Blown aside by the bomb blast?*
> *The fingers of flame came in no time*
> *I struggle but there's only sand, I struggle but there's only sand*
> *One lung was crushed by the ceiling*
> *Left alone like this, where will I float?*
> *I wait for an extended hand*
> *Here I am, here I am*

I want to escape this blood-bathed school
With my girlish eyes still open wide
I know this is my last breath
I am fed up with the roar of the bombs
The sea has raised its clenched fist

Morning is the time we count the dead
On the TV news, in the embassies, in the community centers
In the rubble that was once our buildings and our mosques
Possess us all the more, Amenouzume-san
The morning is still not enough
The morning is still not enough
The morning is still not enough
Dance for us all the more, Amenouzume-san
Claw the milk from your breast, shake your hair wildly
Pound your feet on the ground
And dance
Spin your arms round, shake off your sweat
Bend back your neck
And dance, dance
More
More
Sway your spine, lift your legs
Shake your hips
More
More
Set your womanly shadow on fire
Open your womanly shadow
And call for them
And dance for them
And possess them
And gather
The dead
To the shadow

Give them to morning
Give us morning
The time we count the corpses

WHEN THE MOON RISES

It is the night shift in an abandoned spinning factory
There is only a single light bulb here
The spools of thread turn by themselves
Click goes the bobbins
Changed by the machines
It has already been a decade
Since this place shut down
But when the moon rises, it begins to work
Its strange automation
They say soon after the war
A factory worker's hair got tangled
In the machines, killing her
There are things that float here
But this is not the work of ghosts
No
In the factory
There are peculiar habits
That is what I mean
Peculiar habits remain here
An old lady who spun thread
For forty-four years here
Still licks her index finger and twists
Even on her deathbed
She cannot escape that gesture
That must be true in the netherworld too
Since threads are so infinitely thin
The gestures sink into the bodies
Of those who manipulate the machines
They possess them
Look
How the raw silk thread
Is pulled smoothly

From the factory woman's fingers
Then dances endlessly
The factory is that way too
The axle of the spinning wheel
Remembers
The molecules of steel
Hang their heads in the
Direction in which they spin
Then get caught up
Clanging emptily
When the moonlight pours in
It is not just the tide that is full

Emptily
        Emptily
The spinning wheels spin
The threads swim
Through the abandoned factory

CLUSTERS OF FALLING STARS

Just how many millions of e-mails
Could have been deleted?

★

The dye factory that Asako's father had owned was put up for auction
Two months after the change in leadership
At the branch office of the bank
It was the rules of the free market
That had crushed the local factories bound with loans
But she was fourteen when she learned
It was speculation that determined
Which order the hatchet would fall

The golden boy of the day, IT company CEO Horie Takafumi was arrested
Nine months after the change in section chief
At the Special Investigations Unit of the Tokyo Prosecutor's Office
It was the rules of the Security Exchange Law
That had governed the price fixing of company stocks
But Asako thought it was speculation that determined
Which order the hatchet would fall

"You can sweat but still don't get ahead," her father had said
"You can buy people's hearts with money," Horie had said
"I want to expose a case that'll enrage all of you who sweat for a living," the section chief had said
              In the end, with this arrest,
          Did they investigate
        The companies swollen
     From buying up other corporations
With the speed the investigation deserved?

She heard that well over a hundred computers and cell phones
  were collected
She heard that was because all the important transactions were
  done by e-mail
She heard that two hours before the police came in it was
  leaked to the news
She heard that the investigators were fretting that most of the
  evidence was gone
She heard that some of it had already been disposed of

Just how many millions of e-mails
Could have been deleted?
Asako thinks to herself
Perhaps an astronomical number
They must have deliberately hit delete countless times
So the e-mails would never be found again
It must have been quite the busy week
For the company which fortunately avoided
Being number one on the speculation block

*

What do you wish for
When wishing upon a shower
Of falling electric stars?
She heard Horie once wrote
"Number One in the World"
On a card for Tanabata
If you look up
Right there
Tonight once again
There will be the flashes of another
Huge cluster of falling stars

BACKYARD

A citrus tree stands there
Half rotten, half sprouting new stems
Like a tongue that clings to light
It rattles dryly
A lizard with lovely bluish purple stripes
Dashes across the fallen leaves
And stops abruptly
The buds of the angelica tree
With their curled tails
Quickly grow fluff into thorns and bend back leaves
At some point grandmother appears beside me
"Watch out! If it stings you
It'll hurt for ten whole days"

I gaze at the ants transporting their food
Wondering if they are invisible foam bubbling from the earth
Dislocated and crawling, dislocated and crawling
Looking down on them
They toil so busily
Wriggling as a transparent creature
A wet, earthy aroma fills the air
From the corner of the yard
A butterbur stretching its neck among the ferns
Has probably let out its sigh
The lizard scurries across the threshold of the cleaned out storeroom

The rocks are warm
The thin weight of sleepiness crawls up the back of my neck
Everything grows light before my eyes
"Give the plants some water"
Stretching toward me is a high-pitched voice

That curves gently to the left like a bent bow
I run across the backyard

I run
Across the backyard
The chrysanthemums were planted
The bulges of grandmother's fingers
Had hollowed out the dirt around the roots
"It will grow bigger"
I had watered it and
The leaves had fluttered
Beside the fox god's shrine
A little bird bends in the air
As if its feet were being tickled
It chases
It has intercourse
The tone of its warbling is as if
It is raining though the sun is out
From the shade of the large locust tree
A child looks this way through her narrow eyes

Dig in the dirt
I just wanted to dig in the dirt
Perhaps I was just being dull, perhaps strong and steady
A citrus tree stands there
Half rotten, half sprouting new stems
Like a tongue that clings to light
Before long
The heavy machinery will come
Before we see summer
This lot will be vacant

Dig in the dirt
I just wanted to dig in the dirt

My right shoulder throbs
A white moth flits by
And the skin inside
My muddy boots
Suddenly goes cold

COLORED GLASS

I'll raise it in my tummy
I'll break it
Squashing the bitter worm in my teeth
If I swallow it down
I doubt I'll spit out a moth
Or that it'll fly out as a butterfly
I suppose it'll stay a silkworm spitting out silk forever

    Maybe it'll become a spinning wheel turning its own neck
      The axle letting out a rhythmic rattle under the sawtooth roof
    Its arm extended as it turns itself
Its knees shaking ever so slightly

I'll swallow it down
The silkworm
Down the well of my throat
Where it rebounds in the pit of my stomach
This little worm will spit out a lifeline
And crawl from the watery depths
Forgetting its dreams of flying through the air

    In this strange factory, the worm spins at the spinning wheel
      The raw silk thread winding around before our eyes
    The scissors slip in, and it is bound up tightly
Pulse throbbing from the effort

Warawara   *Are you inviting the thread?*
     Carried away
Somosomo   *Are you touching the thread?*
     Laughed at
Sawasawa   *Are you lining up the thread?*
     Slandered

Moshimoshi   *Are you resentful of the thread?*
  Forgotten
  Extolled
  Untold
Sing: *Roll your hands*   *round and round*   *pull your eyes flat*
     Roll your hands   *round and round*   *pull your eyes flat*
     Roll your hands   *round and round*   *pull your eyes out*

I swallowed it!
The eternal silkworm
On its mission forever
Crawling through the labyrinth of my bowels
The bitter worm squashed in my teeth
In the rustling thread it spins
It ties itself up
Withdraws
And sleeps

It cannot sleep,
I cannot sleep,
Sing: *Roll your hands*   *round and round*   *pull your eyes flat*
     Roll your hands   *round and round*   *pulled my eyes out*
I hold it over my head

> There is a factory floating like an isle inside
> It head turns round and round
> While the blind silkworms glow
> Under the colored glass window

FROM *BEDS AND LOOMS* (2013)

BEDS AND LOOMS

My job was as an operator, to call people out
An inexperienced girl like me
Pick up the receiver, run to the factory floor
And among the noise of looms—*clackity-clack, clackity-clack*
Stand up straight and shout into the women's ears
"*Sat-chan, telephone!*"

The call that day was for Yai-chan
   I dashed through the place
  Where we punch the cards for the looms
Through where we prepare the threads for the warp
There, where we spin the thread, I saw a pornographic picture on
    the calendar
Like in a public path, breasts exposed
In a factory where all but the two who fixed the looms were women
They would let the real thing spill over as well
If a baby cries, you've got to let them feed
The women working in the factory
Put their children on their back, carried them to the cribs
They were saving their money
The oil of the machines, the oil of their hair, the breast milk
Those were the scents of the factory
I hated it, didn't want to breathe them in
Baby beds and power looms, baby beds plus power looms, baby beds
    as power looms
Clackity-clack, clackity-clack, clackity-clack, clackity-clack

The call was for Yai-chan
She had a reputation for her weaving
To finish weaving a bright red robe for a priest

You need a good hand, good eyes, a good mind, a good vagina
It won't work if she doesn't, if she's not a woman among women
The woman manager would always say
     Those priests, never knowing a woman
   It's not Buddhist recitations that let them reach Nirvana
  It's our woman weavers
 It's the robes against their skin that calm their desires
Yai-chan's hand is the oar, rowing on the River of Three Hells
The gold-threaded brocade (four hundred thousand yen per meter)
Worn by the abbot of the high temple
Supported
The life of the factory
The twenty-two workers, their husband's liquor
Their mother-in-law's incense
Their savings for their sons' trips at school

Yai-chan also had a child
With the delivery boy from the noodle shop
Who kept his wife in the country a secret
Their relationship broke off, like noodles cooked to mush
In the stewing stomach of her anger
She gave the baby to her older sister and her husband
So that's why
Even though she was past thirty and her breasts were swollen full
Not a single drop came out, nipples bound up tight
That's why the pornographic picture in the woman's factory by the
Baby beds and power looms, baby beds plus power looms, baby beds
   as power looms
Was an overripe icon of Yai-chan, she who had no one to give her milk
The woman manager would say,
    "The worries that cause her to crease her brow
   Are what make her work late into the night
  Are what make her a woman among women
 We put our hands together in thanks"

Not a very considerate thing to say

My job was to call people out

Yai-chan was farthest back
If the caller got impatient and hung up
We would have to call back at our cost, factory accounts
    determined my speed
I ran, I ran
   I ran as fast as I could
In the place where we stored the thread, piled with spools
I noticed something, something flat
Clackity-clack, clackity-clack, the machines were moving by
    themselves
She was not there
The Maria-Kannon of the Weaving Factory was not there
She was not standing there
She was asleep, she was in bed
  She'd hauled in a double bed!
    Yai-chan had been doing it
      During the lunch breaks with Shō-yan who fixed the looms
The femurs before her sacred gate
Must have *creeeeeeaked*
   As they opened

    (Who can say a baby bed was acceptable
     But a double bed was not?
      The factory worshipped Yai-chan's skill
    If in this woman among women
  We had a secret buddha
 Who could say
She should not open her shrine?
Her loom weaves the robes
Clackity-clack, clackity-clack

The phoenixes in pure gold thread
   Unfold line
   By line
Their combs fall forth like plumes, their claws sharpen
They dance up
In the patterns upon the back and sleeves of the priestly satin robes
The open eyes of the cloud dragon, long whiskers of the rising
   dragon, scales covering the mystic dragon
Dance down
To the birthplace of the thread
Where they intertwine
With the thread
To breathe in the sweat of the rustling sheets
From the double bed found there
The dragons, phoenixes, and lip-licking priests

Clackity-clack, clackity-clack, clackity-clack, clackity-clack
Double bed is a power loom, double bed as a power loom, double
   bed with a power loom
The woman manager
Foamed at the mouth in anger and
To this day still recites the Heart Sutra
Before the shrine of her ancestors

Clackity-clack, clackity-clack, clackity-clack, clackity-clack
Form itself is emptiness, Emptiness itself is form
Sex itself is emptiness, Emptiness itself is sex

   Call them out

   Be called out

   Women are called out

GALAPAGOS

Just gossip! The damn economy is
Just a fairy tale! Stock prices,
Come on and do it!
   Make fun of them all the more
I'm sick of it
All this goth clothing, all this Uniqlo-ing

It's a mess! Eros
Left out all the time! Thanatos
Bring it back to life!
   Alienate them all the more
Incessant cellphones
Microsoft monsters

> *Isn't that all you'd ever let us wear?*
> *Wasn't that our national uniform?*
> *Before the quake*
> *The tsunami of the recession*
> *All we ever worried about?*

That
Is our protective wear
It thrives on adversity
It can withstand high waves
Up to six meters tall
No
It's more like swimming gear
It looks like it might drown
In the cold global
Womb of grotesque globalism
In Lehman Brothers
Salaried men

Don't want anything
Don't say anything
Won't do anything, won't do it anymore
Girls, boys, the intermediate sex
Not more procreating, unisex
  Just look
    At that fission
They say they can't get any fusion
Between those sperm-like neutrons

It's just been let go! Nuclear fission
Just exposed! The womb of the reactor dome too
Fuel rods (*nenryōbō*), safety hats (*anzenbō*), egg cells (*ransaibō*),
    stinginess (*kechinbō*), thieves (*dorobō*),
Refrigerators (*reibō*), heaters (*danbō*),
Babies (*akanbō*), deceased (*butsunbō*), floating (*ukabō*) on the great
    plain of the sea, on the verge of screaming (*orabō*),
The reactor building about to fly off (*buttobō*),
Embankments (*teibō*), conspiracies (*inbō*), ministerial offices
    (*kanbō*),
      Unbelievabō
    Incredibō
TEPCO
    Puts on their Uniqlo
    To bulwark
The tsunami

      No nuclear dome
     We'll make electricity
    In our con-domes
  Is a half-life
Good enough?

Us

HALF A PAIR OF SHOES

the red poppy is in bloom
a leather shoe, just half a pair,
lies washed up on the seashore
laces still tied

as the poppy bends
and drops dew from its petals
the shoe sighs faintly
the flower shakes itself off
and the dirty shoe
starts to open
its eye

mostly likely
no landscapes are reflected
in that eye, deep as an old well,
memories
soak through
the poppy can only caress
she extends her leaves
toward the chest-like instep

>   —*You cannot break me, the waves*
>   *cannot wash away*
>   *my worn-down heel*
>   *and my folds*

  they draw near
  the gaze of the shoeless boy
  going as far as the water's edge
if the poppy gazed in
how clear that eye would be

a fire, like a small fish's fin
at the bottom of an old well

>   —*The sea cannot extinguish*
>   *the frank, pale flame*
>   *at the depths of my existence*
>   *for the sea too is an enormous eye*

   what light must the wave have emitted
  in that moment
 as it watered and rushed
surging in anger
far from shore
as the other shoe was swallowed

>   —*Did the school of sardines*
>   *see the circle*
>   *of blue flame*
>   *drawn in my eyes?*

the poppy is trembling again
no
it is the wind
the flower stands naked
dropping its petals
into the well

it is an umbilical cord
the tip of the shoelace
falling into the depths of the eye
where the boy tries to grab on

down it crawls

LOTS AND LOTS

Tsutomu and Isamu—
Those names were popular among boys back then
But we weren't even paying attention when
One of Osamu's creations, our number one author,
Crossed the sea and changed
His name to Astro
Hmmmm… Think about it
   To tell the truth
It didn't even come across as some cruel joke
When Atom
The boy hero came calling
From the islands where the atomic bombs once fell

When did we realize
What his name really meant?
Hmmmm… Think about it
I wanted to be friends with Uran
This is no cruel joke
All of us kids were that way back then
Each one of us with an atomic reactor in our hearts
Maybe we were the ones who changed his name
Calling him
Atom

When we called him that
We cut off
The root
Of the word
For the future, for the universe
For our own peaceful uses, as a nation that had suffered through
   the bomb
I don't want to blame

The young Tezuka
The adults wanting to sell dreams
The children wanting to lose themselves in dreams
Went right along too
With his inklings and the iron-arms
Like filings to a magnet
Lots of them

And lots of them
He would not have been able to draw him
If that were really his name
He could not depict him as *Genko*, a girl robot
That was what we needed
  Right then
A new nuance
For the future, for the universe
For our twisted peace
The name "Atom"
Split off of the atom
And the atomic bomb

  —The reason his power source
  Was swept out to sea one day
  Was because it was not included
  It had been cut off from the start
      The language on these islands
    Gets rid of roots, cuts them off with katakana
  Long before the earthquake
      If so, then

It was okay to use that name
      So that's why
    His name, all sparkling clean
Was used

Lots
And lots
Until smeared with filth and mud

What we have are not fifty-four reactors
We have fifty-four Atoms standing there at the water's edge
Of the four that the waves swallowed
Three blew themselves up, one's innards failed
The jets in their legs
Rained down iodine, cesium, strontium
His little brother Cobalt chased after him
Through fields, mountains, towns
    Among people, livestock, butterflies
The furnaces in the three Atoms' hearts
Melted down and collapsed
    Making
His little sister Uran seethe, the fission wouldn't stop
Professor Ochanomizu and Dr. Tenma were killed
Into the sea poured
An accumulation of tears
From his kind heart
Some of the other Atoms
Also stood atop fault lines
Some grew old, their metallic exhaustion began
And then
Even though we shut them down
We still couldn't find a place to get rid of them
This is our one and only world
Not a manga in which we can blow things up in space
    There he was
Mulling over the laws of robotics
"I was born to make people happy"
Perhaps all this hurt him more than humanity

*

At the edge of the water
Fifty-four severed heads
Four of them
Eyes lowered, noses lowered, piling upon penance day after day
One lowering countless children of science on a land of withered trees
One killing countless children of science in a sea without salt or moon
One surprised as it measures the dead Atom's legs and the living Atom's eyes
On its scale of tangled serpents only to find they weigh the same
One dead and still sicker than before
Coughing within its concrete sarcophagus

*

A single butterfly crosses the Becquerel Straits.

*

A face appears below the ground
The sad face of a sick man
The grass sprouts and sways
Countless hairs begin to tremble
From the sad, sick surface
The sad face of Atom appears
Tears dripping
Dripping tears
   At this moment
Thin roots
Hairy roots
Cilia from root tips

Cilia covered in faint hair

They will grow, won't they?
We will make them grow, won't we?
In the soil that is the language of these islands
In the deep darkness at its base

An object mired in karma
   Will he ever
      Be allowed
To rest in peace?

SPECTER!

There is a girl who goes nowhere
There is a girl who sucks up severe nourishment
Like a water jug
Deep in my eyes
I illuminate
Things buried in the earth
I can see them
I can see
Gossamer shimmering illusions
Inside my body
If I close my eyes

There is a girl with roots
Could one call her lonely?
Certainly the gossamer shimmering
Under the earth does not speak
Does not touch her breasts
They simply gush
Stick up and shine, shatter into seven colors
    And that is where I sew
Like a freshwater fish
I forget myself
And travel
Still rooted
Unable to budge
I grow

How many hands
Will stick out?
Mother and father
Many mothers and fathers
Fly about and warble

I will
    Forget
        My forgotten
            Time

If the gossamer illusions
Rise up to fill the girl's fingers
Flowers will adhere to them
These first
Colors
Are what the buried ones have resigned us to

Look!
No
Close your eyes
The rustling buds
That are beginning to swell
Stroke them
    Softly
Moisten your ring finger
With a little spit

        It's running! Look,
           The specter
              Is running
           Through your eyes
         Across your floor
      The girl and her gossamer illusions
    Attagirl!
Look, above your head too

"Springtime, come to us!"

UNCOLLECTED POEMS

SHADOWS

In this place suddenly thrown into disarray
It is impossible to distinguish
Between what is garbage
What is not and what is still useable
So much earth, sand and dust
Has fallen that
Everywhere I see
A great can of refuse
The mucus I wipe on my sleeve is black
The throat and the lungs are eroded
Let it be, just the way it is…
Listless and resigned, I roll up my sleeves
And muster what little enthusiasm I can

I cannot let this be turned into a vacant lot
At least until I pick up the marble
I dropped here before it became this way
At least until I can pick through the refuse
And save at least one suitcase's worth of junk

It will be completely stripped away
It will disappear
I must stretch out my hands
And hold fast to
The shadows of this land
In a suitcase I will surely
Never open again

TRANSLATOR'S NOTES

ITŌ HIROMI

Coyote: Itō's grandmother was a shamaness who claimed to speak to the dead, and Itō's mother taught her children small, magical spells. This poem explores the mystical connection between Itō and the various generations of women in her family. The second stanza of "Coyote" derives its inspiration from the German performance artist Joseph Beuys. In 1974, he came to New York and immediately installed himself in a gallery, where he remained in a small room with a coyote for three days. Beuys later explained, "I wanted to isolate myself, insulate myself, see nothing of America other than the coyote." Through forging a spiritual connection with this animal, which Native Americans had believed to be divine, Beuys hoped to come to start the process of making amends for the destruction waged upon the culture and environment of the Native Americans. The exchange between the coyote and the daughter in the poem contains a bastardized quote from *The Heart Sutra* (*Hannya shingyō*), a short Buddhist sutra which some sects believe to express the essential concepts of the religion. The sutra concludes with a mantra, which if read in Japanese, states *"Gyatei gyatei haragyatei harasōgyatei boji sowaka"* (Gone, gone, to the other shore, gone, reach, accomplish enlightenment). In the poem, the coyote and the daughter do not repeat the excerpt from *The Heart Sutra* accurately. If anything, it becomes a symbol of a sort of mysterious, mystical exchange between them.

Vinegar, Oil: This poem draws inspiration from Haga Noboru's book *A History of Funeral Rites (Sōgi no rekishi)*. Many of the things that Itō lists in the italicized passages are the sorts of things for which one might pray at local temples. For instance, one might pray for long life, love, and divine protection against moles or severe ailments. Moreover, the "belt-removal temple" (*Obitoke-dera*) in Nara is well known as a place to offer prayers for a child, and many people come to the "thorn-removing Jizō" (*togenuki Jizō*) near Itō's former home in Sugamo, Tokyo to pray for cures to their ailments. The "Tofu Jizō" (*Tōfu Jizō*) is a statue of the Buddhist deity Jizō located in the Shinjuku ward of Tokyo, and the "Falling-off horses Jizō" (*Rakuba Jizō*) is located near Waseda in Tokyo. The reference to "malt candy" has to do with a special candy known as "ghost child-rearing candy" (*yōrei kosodate ame*) in eastern Kyoto. According to folklore, there was a ghost who came to a particular shop everyday to buy candy to feed her child, who was still alive. Nearby the shop that still sells this candy is a statue of Jizō dedicated to child rearing.

The Heart Sutra: After the year 2000, Itō experienced a series of deaths in her immediate family, first her mother, then her father, then the dog that she had cared for over many years and most recently her life partner in California. Around the same time, Itō became interested in the classical Buddhist texts, with their accounts of suffering, aging, and dying. This translation comes from a collection in which she retranslates these classical Chinese texts into modern Japanese along with her own personal commentary. As mentioned in the notes to the earlier poem "Coyote," *The Heart Sutra (Hannya shingyō)* is one of the most well known Buddhist texts in Japan, and this contemporary rendition, which she frequently reads at public poetry readings, represents her interpretation of it. In translating the text, instead of turning back to the original Chinese, I have relied on Itō's contemporary Japanese translation in order to showcase her individual interpretation.

Yakisoba: Since moving to California in the mid-1990s, Itō has been interested in the lives of *Nikkeijin* (the Japanese diaspora) and the complex relationships that Japanese-Americans have with

Japan. This and the following handful of poems are products of that interest. The first quotation, with its idiosyncratic mixture of Japanese and English means something like "Hey lady, take a look! *Good sauce* is *included*!" The second quotation means something like, "Wow, this is *rather cheap*, isn't it?" The lines "All of the what / That are there?" are a reference to a famous haiku by Natsume Sōseki, written on the occasion of the funeral of Otsuka Naoko, a married author for whom he bore a special love. The poem reads, "All the chrystanthemums / that are there, throw them / Inside the coffin."

Eels and Catfish: This poem was inspired by a visit made by the Japanese-American poet Brandon Shimoda to Kumamoto, the area from which his ancestors came and where Itō's second home is located. She spends a significant portion of each year there.

Anpanman and Johnnies: Japanese schools, like the one described in this poem, can be found in many international cities that have a high number of Japanese and Japanese-American residents. The one that inspired this poem is located in San Diego, not far from Encinitas, California where Itō resides. Anpanman is a popular Japanese animated cartoon for children. Johnnies is the name for a management company that produces many of the young male pop idols in Japan.

Mother Dies: In 2010, it was discovered that all throughout Japan, there were a large number of centenarians who were reported as still being alive but who had really passed away. In those cases, the families were continuing to collect the pensions of the deceased, rather than going through the trouble to transfer the pension into their own name. In some cases, they had even covered up the corpse or disposed of it. Tawada Yōko, who is mentioned briefly in the poem, is a writer and poet who has been living and working in Germany for the last couple of decades.

Cooking, Writing Poetry: This poem was written for the one-year anniversary of the 2011 earthquake, tsunami, and Fukushima meltdown. As mentioned in the introduction, Itō uses this poem—an "anti-poem" in her words—as a way to comment on the flood of poetic production in the wake of the disasters. In the wake of the disasters, all advertisements were pulled from Japanese television and replaced with a public service announcement containing a poem by the early twentieth-century poet Kaneko Misuzu urging people to be kind to one another in the face of adversity. This announcement appeared so frequently on television that it became one of the enduring memories of many people in Japan who lived through the disasters. This poem, in Itō's opinion, was like the flood of poetry produced after 2011, much too clichéd and simplistic to deal with the enormous human catastrophe on the ground. Itō also mentions a poem by an American poet, namely J.D. McClatchy's poem "One Year Later," published in *March Was Made of Yarn* (Vintage International, 2012). Jeffrey Angles rendered McClatchy's poem into Japanese for inclusion in a Japanese-language edition of the same collection, and showed it to Itō in order to get her opinion. One sees in this poem that although she did not personally like the poem much, she admired him for trying to deal with the disasters through language, the strongest tool a poet has at hand.

HIRATA TOSHIKO

Lemons: In Japanese, the two most common ways to write the word meaning *lemon* are in the phonetic katakana syllabary (レモン, pronounced *remon*) and in kanji (檸檬, pronounced *reimou* or *remon*). Even though both options mean the same thing, the kanji are quite difficult and dense, and thus give the word a heavier, weightier feeling than the phonetic representation, which is relatively accessible and light. Kajii Motojirō (1901-1932) was a modernist writer from Kyoto best known for his short story "The Lemon," which is still taught in many Japanese high schools. Takamura Kōtarō (1883-1956) is an important early twentieth-century poet best known for his poems about his wife Chieko (1886-1938), who suffered a mental collapse, attempted suicide, and eventually died in her psychiatric ward of tuberculosis. In this poem, Hirata is accusing Kōtarō, who could sometimes be overbearing, of manipulating the material in his Chieko poems in ways that made the experience more about him than her.

Morning Illusions: In Japan, calendars often make reference to auspicious or unlucky dates. *Tsuchinoe* means "the fifth of the ten Chinese calendar signs" and *shakkō* indicates a mostly unlucky day during which one's sole stroke of luck is likely to come at noon. (The word *tsuchinoe,* written phonetically in Hirata's poem, is a homonym for the words meaning "dirt pictures," whereas the word *shakkō* is written with characters meaning "red mouth." Both words might seem oddly intriguing for a child who isn't aware of the tradition of fortune telling.) The rest of Hirata's poem revolves around misreadings of characters. For instance, if one reverses the characters in the word *hachimitsu* or "honey" (蜂蜜), one will get the word *mitsubachi* or "honeybee" (蜜蜂). As Hirata points out, the characters for the word *shinsō* or "truth" (真相) look like the characters for "prime minister" (首相). The magazine *Rumored Truths* was an anti-political tabloid published from 1979 to 2004.

At Some Point Things Get Rough: This poem contains several associations based on sound. The word for "line" *(sen)* is a homonym for the final part of the verb ending *–masen*, which negates the term. Hirata works the kanji meaning "line" into to the two lines that follow the long ellipsis. Although reproducing this word play in English is near impossible, in order to at least hint that it was there in the original, I've added the English play on words, "a *line* of dots hinting along those *lines*." In Japanese sound of the verb "stab in the back" (*uragiru*) is reminiscent the name Urashima Tarō, who is a Rip van Winkle-like figure from Japanese folklore. According to the story, Urashima Tarō travels to the bottom of the sea and spends what seems like only a few days there, but when he tries to return home, he finds that hundreds of years have passed on earth.

ARAI TAKAKO

Soul Dance: This poem was written at the time of the Iraq War and the 2004 tsunami in the Indian Ocean. In an interview for the journal *Full Tilt,* Arai commented, "Every morning, I would wake up, turn on the TV or open the newspaper only to find reports of the numbers of the dead… It seems so ironic to see such terrible tragedies and cruelty transposed into numbers. At the same time, I wanted to try to depict the mornings that surrounded those huge and weighty numbers." Amenouzume is a mythical Japanese goddess associated with dance and performance. Through her dance, she is said to have lured the Sun Goddess Amaterasu out of a rock cave where she had secluded herself, thus plunging the world into darkness. The words "womanly shadow" that appear toward the end of the poem is a euphemism for the vagina.

Clusters of Falling Stars: In this poem, Arai refers to the collapse of the textile industry of her own hometown of Kiryū in Gunma Prefecture, as well as the arrest of the young CEO and television personality Horie Takafumi. Horie's company Livedoor had bought up massive amounts of stock in media-related companies, so when he was arrested for securities fraud in 2006, it became a national media event. *Tanabata*, sometimes called the "Star Festival" in English, is held during the summer. On that day, people write their wishes on long cards and hang them on a spring of bamboo.

Colored Glass: The poem represents the author's reaction to the collapse of the silk and textile industry in her hometown of Kiryū in Gunma Prefecture, once a major Japanese center of textile production. In this poem, Arai imagines a person swallowing a silkworm, which begins to grow and creates its own silk factory inside her stomach. The poem was inspired by the Japanese expression "*Nigamushi o kamitubusu*" (literally "to squash a bitter bug in your teeth"), which is used to describe someone's expression when they are making a frown or grimace. Many of the textile factories in Kiryū had roofs that zigzag up and down like the teeth on a saw, hence the phrase "saw tooth roof" (*nokogiri-yane*) used in the poem. Glass windows would then be placed on one side of each "tooth" of the roof to let in light. In the final stanza, Arai imagines a mini-silk factory floating in the narrator's stomach, the colored glass in the saw tooth roof illuminating the interior. The lines "roll your hands, round and round, pull your eyes flat" (*kaiguri kaiguri totto no me*) are from a children's game. The child rolls their hands around one another as if they are rolling up thread on their hands like a spinning wheel, then after that, they pull at the corner of their eyes. Arai creates a variation on this song, imagining that the narrator pulls her own eyes out.

Beds and Looms: -*Chan* is a diminutive suffix used after a person's name or sometimes the first-syllable of a person's name in order to show affection toward them. -*Yan* is another diminutive suffix, used in Gunma dialect, to attach to a man's name. The remainder of the poem contains a number of references to Japanese Buddhist culture. In Japan, Buddhist priests typically wear beautifully woven, ornately patterned robes requiring a high level of skill, and that is one of the types of material that was woven in the town of Kiryū. The "River of the Three Hells" is the river separating the world of the living from the world of the dead in Buddhist mythology. The reference to "Maria-Kannon" comes from premodern era, when Christianity was prohibited in Japan. During that time, a small minority of "hidden Christians" clung to their beliefs and used Buddhist images as an outlet for their beliefs. For instance, they used the image of Kannon, the Buddhist goddess of mercy, as an image of the Christ's mother Mary. The words "secret buddha" *(hibutsu)* are a euphemism for a woman's genitals. "Form itself is emptiness, Emptiness itself is form" is a line from *The Heart Sutra*, one of the principal texts of Japanese Buddhism.

Galapagos: This and the following two poems were written after the 2011 disasters in northeastern Japan. The title comes from the fact that commentators on the Japanese economy sometimes compare Japan to the Galapagos, the isolated group of Ecuadorian islands where developments frequently veer off in their own unique directions, different from those of the rest of the world. This poem also comments on serious issues—the ongoing anxiety about the Japanese economy during the ongoing nuclear crisis at Fukushima, concern about the extremely low national birthrate, and even the lack of individuality of Japanese youth. In referring to the low national birth rate, Arai jokes that Japan does not have much "fusion" of sperm and ova; instead what the Japanese population has is mostly "fission"—the breaking apart of radioactive isotopes in the Fukushima meltdown. In this work, Arai pokes fun at the discriminatory idea, circulated in the popular media and on blogs, that young people from the polluted areas ought to consider using condoms rather than having unprotected sex for fear that radiation might have had long-term, unpredictable effects on them and their progeny. In commenting on this poem, Arai has mentioned that she wanted to show that the tendency in Japan to put economics first led not only to the nuclear accident; it also has brought people to a point where they feel compelled to limit their own freedoms and joy. In the middle of the poem, Arai lines up a number of words that all end with the syllable *bō*. As she watched the press coverage of the Fukushima meltdown, she was surprised that so many of the items filling the news ended with the same sound.

Lots and Lots: This poem was inspired by the books *This is How We Choose to Be a "Nuclear Power" (Watashi-tachi wa kōshite "genpatsu ōkoku" o eranda)* by Takeda Tōru and *The Atomic Energy We Dreamed of (Yume no genshiryoku)* by Yoshimi Shun'ya. Both books talk about the ways in which the Japanese population was desensitized to the idea of atomic power in the postwar period. Takeda points to the role of the popular manga artist Tezuka Osamu (1928-1989), whose wildly popular comic character "Iron-Armed Atom" *(Tetsuwan Atomu)* suggested to the Japanese population that nuclear power could be used for good. The character's name was changed to "Astro Boy" when the animated feature based on this comic was first exported to the United States. Atom's little sister is named Uran (from the word "Uranium") and his younger brother "Cobalt." Throughout this poem, Arai uses Tezuka's character "Atom" as a stand-in for the fifty-four nuclear stations located throughout Japan. Regarding the names that Arai mentions in the first stanza, Tsutomu means "strong" or "dedicated," while Isamu means "brave." Both names were popular during the 1950s when the manga artist Tezuka Osamu was at work on Astro Boy. Professor Ochanomizu and Dr. Tenma are characters that appear in Tezuka's manga. In the fourth stanza, Arai suggests that in the male-dominated era of the 1950s, Tezuka did not want to create a female robot. To avoid gender confusion, he used the English word "Atom" to name his character instead of using the Japanese equivalent. The reason is that the word meaning "atom" in Japanese is written 原子 *(genshi)*, but since the character 子 *(ko)* appears at the end of many girls' names in contemporary Japan, this name might lead readers to assume the character was female.

ACKNOWLEDGEMENTS

The translator would like to thank Itō, Hirata, and Arai for their friendship, cooperation, and support over the years. It is a thrill to bring together for the first time, the work of these three provocative poets into a single volume.

The translator is also especially grateful to Ishiuchi Miyako, the world-renowned feminist photographer who allowed us to use her photograph on the cover of this volume. The photograph comes from the collection *sa-bo-ten* (Yamato Press, 2013). One reason we chose this image by Ishiuchi is because the cactus is tough, prickly, and able to thrive in harsh environments, much like the strong, smart, tough poets in this collection.

A second reason is that Ishiuchi is also a close friend of all three poets. In 1995, Ishiuchi published a collection of nude photographs of Itō Hiromi called *Hands-Legs-Flesh-Body—Hiromi 1955 (Te-ashi-niku-karada—Hiromi 1955)*, and ten years later in 2005, she published *Scars (Kizuato)*, which included photographs of Hirata Toshiko's back and arms. By coincidence, both Ishiuchi and Arai were born in the same textile town of Kiryū, and so when Arai published her third book of poetry *Beds and Looms* in 2013, she used one of Ishiuchi's photographs of a woman's kimono on the cover. Thank you to Ishiuchi and to her assistant Tomoka Aya for providing a high-quality scan.

Some of the translations in this collection were published in early versions in the following journals and books. Thank you to the various editors and publishers for their support and willingness to allow me to update and publish the translations in this volume.

ITŌ HIROMI

Killing Kanoko: Selected Poems of Hiromi Itō (Action Books, 2009): "Coyote," "Vinegar, Oil," "Father's Uterus, Or the Map," "Marjoram, Dill, Rosemary"; *Poetry Salzburg:* "The Heart Sutra," "Mother Dies," "Anpanman and Johnnies"; *Granta:* "Yakisoba";

Evening Oracle (Letter Machine Editions, 2015): "Eels and Catfish"; *These Things Here and Now: Poetry Responses to the March 11, 2011 Disasters* (Josai University Press, 2016): "Cooking, Writing Poetry"

HIRATA TOSHIKO

Action Yes: "Greetings are Important," "My Fun Family," "Complaints from the Inhabitant," "Weird," "P-E-O-P-L-E," "Man Without Arms," "Van Gogh's *Bedroom* as I See It; *Connotations Press:* "Beautiful Staples"; *The White Review:* "Camera," "The Cat Stays Even After It's Gone, and I Cast My Suspicions on It"; *Words Without Borders:* "Do Not Tremble; *These Things Here and Now: Poetry Responses to the March 11, 2011 Disasters* (Josai University Press, 2016): "Do Not Tremble," "Cold Spring"

ARAI TAKAKO

Soul Dance: Selected Poems of Takako Arai (Mi'Te Press, 2008): "Give Us Morning," "When the Moon Rises," "Backyard," "Shadows"; *Octopus:* "Clusters of Falling Stars," "Colored Glass"; *Southpaw:* "Beds and Looms"; *Poetry Kanto:* "Galapagos," "Half a Pair of Shoes," "Specter!"; *These Things Here and Now: Poetry Responses to the March 11, 2011 Disasters* (Josai University Press, 2016): "Galapagos," "Half a Pair of Shoes," "Lots and Lots"; *Big Bridge:* "Specter!"

www.ingramcontent.com/pod-product-compliance
Lightning Source LLC
Chambersburg PA
CBHW030900170426
43193CB00009BA/690